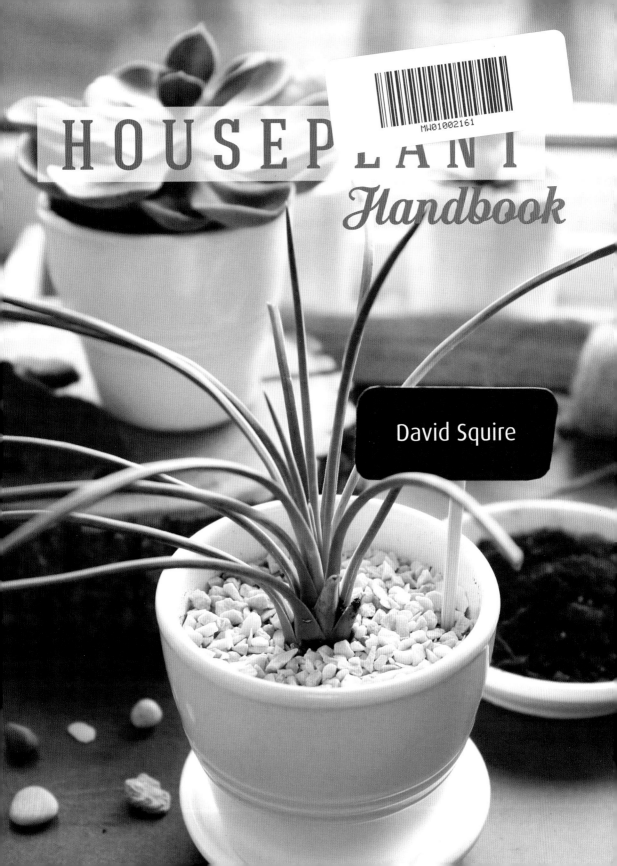

HOUSEPLANT
Handbook

David Squire

Houseplant Handbook

CompanionHouse Books™ is an imprint of Fox Chapel Publishers International Ltd.

Project Team
Editorial Director: Christopher Reggio
Editor: Colleen Dorsey
Copy Editor: Laura Taylor
Design: Mary Ann Kahn
Index: Jay Kreider

ISBN 978-1-62008-232-4

Library of Congress Cataloging-in-Publication Data

Names: Squire, David, 1938- author.
Title: Houseplant handbook / David Squire.
Description: Mount Joy, PA : CompanionHouse Books, [2017] | Includes index.
Identifiers: LCCN 2017032127 | ISBN 9781620082324 (pbk.)
Subjects: LCSH: House plants--Handbooks, manuals, etc.
Classification: LCC SB419 .S642 2017 | DDC 635.9/65--dc23
LC record available at https://lccn.loc.gov/2017032127

This book has been published with the intent to provide accurate and authoritative information in regard to the subject matter within. While every precaution has been taken in the preparation of this book, the author and publisher expressly disclaim any responsibility for any errors, omissions, or adverse effects arising from the use or application of the information contained herein.

Fox Chapel Publishing
903 Square Street
Mount Joy, PA 17552

Fox Chapel Publishers International Ltd.
7 Danefield Road, Selsey (Chichester)
West Sussex PO20 9DA, U.K.

www.facebook.com/companionhousebooks

Printed and bound in Singapore
20 19 18 17   2 4 6 8 10 9 7 5 3 1

CONTENTS

Part One

LOOKING AFTER HOUSEPLANTS

Part Two

PLANT DIRECTORY

Part One

LOOKING AFTER HOUSEPLANTS

KNOW
THE
BASICS

Always check for signs of a healthy plant before you buy from a nursery or garden center.

Each year, the popularity of houseplants increases and few people can resist having some flowering or foliage plants to transform their house into a home. Apart from creating color and vibrancy, houseplants have a therapeutic quality: they are alive and need regular, careful attention, generating rapport with people throughout the year.

Given the fast pace of life today, and the pressure it creates in our lives, the restful atmosphere that can be engendered by houseplants is essential. The range of houseplants is wide, including flowering and foliage types, as well as indoor ferns, bromeliads, cacti and other succulents, palms and cycads, bulbs, and insectivorous plants. All have different needs, and whether your home is a bungalow or a high-rise apartment, there are plants that will thrive in it. Some are native to tropical and subtropical regions, while others are hardy enough to grow outdoors in temperate zones but can also be grown indoors when young and in a pot.

In the directory of houseplants in Part Two (see pages 62–211), you will find detailed information about each plant's needs, from warmth and light throughout the year, to watering and feeding, as well as how to increase plants.

Growing plants indoors is an all-embracing hobby. While some plants happily thrive on windowsills, others develop into large, eye-catching features that live for so long they become as much a part of a home as a dog or cat. Indeed, it is not unknown for long-lived plants to be given pet names!

Looking after houseplants requires skill and dedication because they are such a disparate group, ranging from plants native to deserts to those with a jungle heritage. Some have a limited life span, while others continue their display throughout the year.

BUYING HOUSEPLANTS

Choosing and buying plants for the home needs care if they are to create spectacular displays that last a long time. There are several sources of houseplants, including garden centers, plant nurseries, florists, and main-street shops. Each has advantages, but whatever the source, it is essential to inspect the plant before buying it (see box on page 10).

Getting Your Plant Home

The first stage in ensuring a good display is to get your plant home safely. Here are some hints.

* Either make buying a plant a separate occasion, or the last stop on a shopping expedition.
* In winter, do not put plants in a cold car boot or trunk. Also avoid these areas in summer as they quickly become excessively hot.
* Avoid putting plants in either cold or hot drafts near open windows.

10 TIPS FOR BUYING HOUSEPLANTS

1. Always buy from a reputable source. A cheap purchase may prove expensive if the plant dies a few weeks later.

2. Never buy a houseplant that is displayed outside a shop; in winter, such plants become chilled, while in summer they are exposed to direct, often intense sunlight. Flowering plants suffer most from excessive cold or heat.

3. Avoid buying plants that show signs of pests and diseases (see pages 34–39). They are never a success and may infect houseplants already in your home. Check above and under leaves, as well as on flowers and stems.

This plant needs to be repotted.

4. Never buy a plant with masses of roots growing out of drainage holes in the pot's base. This indicates that the plant has been neglected and needs repotting. Additionally, growth may have been retarded.

5. When buying flowering plants, ensure there are plenty of flower buds waiting to open. Avoid plants that are in full flower—their display will be short-lived.

6. Do not buy plants that are wilting; this indicates neglect from which the plant may not recover.

7. Check that the compost is evenly moist. Plants can wilt through excessive watering as well as from being kept dry.

Moldy compost indicates excessive watering.

8. Avoid buying plants with green mold on the compost's surface; it indicates neglect and excessive watering.

9. Only buy clearly labeled plants, as this indicates a reputable source.

10. Do not buy large plants that are growing in very small pots, or small plants growing in very large pots. Apart from an imbalance of size and a lack of stability, large plants in small pots need frequent watering, while it is difficult to keep the moisture content of the compost of small plants in large pots even and not too wet.

The size of plants and their pots should be in balance.

* Many plant nurseries and garden centers sell houseplants totally covered in a paper wrapper or plastic sleeve to protect them from knocks and cold winds.
* If possible, leave young children and lively dogs at home when shopping for plants!

Acclimatizing Plants to Your Home

As soon as possible, get your plants home and remove the wrappings. If left covered, stems and foliage may become distorted. Here are some ideas on how to establish plants indoors.

* Check that the compost is lightly moist, but not saturated and waterlogged.

Protective sleeve

* Initially, place your plant in a cool or moderately warm room, out of direct and strong sunlight, and away from cold or hot drafts. After a few days, position it in the location with its desired temperature and light intensity (see conditions recommended for individual plants in Part Two).
* If the plant is flowering, avoid bumping it, which may cause buds to fall off.
* If you suspect your plant is contaminated with pests and diseases, isolate and treat it with an insecticide or fungicide (see pages 34–39).

Pots, Saucers, and Cachepots

These are fundamental to growing houseplants. Traditionally, pots were made of clay, and these still are considered ideal for plants, though plastic pots have gained increasing popularity. Both have advantages and disadvantages.

Clay Pots

* ✳ are heavier than plastic pots, creating a firm base for large plants
* ✳ have a porous nature that allows damaging salts from fertilizers to escape—a bonus if plants are excessively fed
* ✳ encourage the compost to remain cool in summer and warm in winter
* ✳ have a natural color that harmonizes with all plants
* ✳ absorb moisture readily, so must be immersed in clean water for a few hours before use
* ✳ usually break when dropped on a hard surface
* ✳ are more difficult to clean than plastic pots when very dirty
* ✳ are more expensive than plastic pots
* ✳ are usually used in conjunction with loam-based composts

Plastic Pots

* ✳ are light and easy to handle
* ✳ are not porous, so plants need less frequent watering than when in clay pots
* ✳ are available in a wide color range
* ✳ do not break easily when dropped, although cold temperatures make them brittle
* ✳ are cheaper than clay pots
* ✳ are usually used in conjunction with soil-less composts, such as those based on peat

Plastic pots

Clay pots

Saucers

These are placed under pots to prevent water draining from the compost and trickling onto decorative surfaces. Most are now made of plastic, in a wide range of colors and sizes. Choose a size fractionally larger than the pot's base.

Saucers

Cachepots

Also known as cover pots and potholders, cachepots are decorative, usually complementing the decor and a plant's flowers and leaves. Some are plain colors, while others are patterned; most are round, others square. The growing pot is placed inside the cachepot. The rim of the growing pot must be level or slightly below that of the cachepot.

The practical difficulty with cachepots is that it is easy to over-water a plant unwittingly. Water remains in the pot's base, eventually causing roots to decay. About 10 minutes after watering a plant, remove the plant, together with its growing pot, and tip away water remaining in the cachepot's base.

Cachepot

Match the cachepot color to the colors of the plant.

Range of Pot Sizes

Pots are measured by the width across the rim, ranging from 2in (5cm) to about 15in (38cm). For home gardeners who buy a plant and discard it when it ages and becomes unsightly, only a few spare pots are needed, but enthusiastic houseplant growers will need a few more so plants can be repotted into larger pots. Ideally, when repotting a plant, especially when small, a pot of only about 1in (25mm) larger than the existing one is about right. However, this would require a wide assortment of pots, so a range of pots, each about 2in (5cm) larger than the next, is usually selected.

POTTING COMPOSTS

Garden soil is unsuitable for growing plants in pots indoors; it has a variable nature and may contain pests, diseases, and weed seeds. Buy special compost mixtures.

Traditionally, loam-based composts were—and still are—used. These are formed of partially sterilized loam, sharp sand (also known as concreting sand), and peat, with the addition of fertilizers and ground limestone or chalk. Never use soft sand (or builders' sand), which compacts when wet and does not allow air to penetrate the compost.

Difficulties in obtaining good loam encouraged the creation of composts without loam, known as soil-less composts. They are formed mainly of mixtures based on granulated peat and are uniform, as well as lighter and cleaner to use than loam-based types. Both have advantages and disadvantages.

Loam-Based Composts

* are heavier than peat-based types, giving greater stability to plants, especially those with a mass of foliage
* are unlikely to dry out as fast or as completely as peat-based types
* have a larger reserve of minor and trace plant foods than peat-based types
* are suitable for most houseplants

UNDERSTANDING THE TERM "COMPOST"

The term compost is often confusing and can be interpreted in several ways. Here are a few terms you might encounter.

Potting composts are free from pests and diseases and are specially formulated to encourage the active growth of roots, providing suitable plant foods, air, and moisture. **All references in this book to "compost" are solely to potting composts**; a range of them is described on pages 14–16.

Loam-based composts are primarily based on partially sterilized loam. For details, see page 14.

Soil-less composts, often known as soil-less compost mixes, are mainly formed of granulated peat and, for that reason, are frequently called peat-based composts (more information on page 16).

Garden compost is derived from organic waste material from gardens and kitchens that has been placed in a compost heap or bin and allowed to decay. Eventually, this material, when fully decayed and friable, is either dug into soil to improved its structure and fertility, or spread on the surface of bare soil or around (but not touching) established plants to increase soil fertility and inhibit the growth of weeds (known as mulching). The decaying process can take up to a year and is influenced by temperature, bacteria activity, air, and moisture. This material is not a suitable compost in which to grow house plants.

Garden soil (sometimes just referred to as potting soil) is not suitable for house plants as it has a variable nature and may contain an imbalance of clay, silt, and loam as well as being contaminated by pests and diseases. It may also be excessively acidic or alkaline and nutritionally imbalanced.

Peat-Based Composts

* are more uniform than loam-based composts
* are easily carried home in bags and stored (seal the bag's top by folding it over)
* are light and easy to use
* dry out more quickly than loam-based types and are more difficult to remoisten if watering is neglected
* require plants to be fed at an earlier stage in their growth than with loam-based composts

Other Types of Compost

The continued removal of peat from peat beds has destroyed the environments of many animals, birds, insects and native plants, so there has been pressure to use more environmentally friendly composts. These are formed of several different materials, some of which are also used as additives to other composts to help retain moisture. Look for peat-free composts when buying soil-less types.

Specialist Composts

The range of plants grown indoors is wide, and it is clear that just one type of compost will not suit them all. Most flowering and foliage houseplants grow well in loam-based or peat-based composts (but do not change the type of compost when repotting a plant). Specialist plants, such as cacti and bromeliads, need types better suited to their specific needs. These can be purchased from garden centers and specialist outlets.

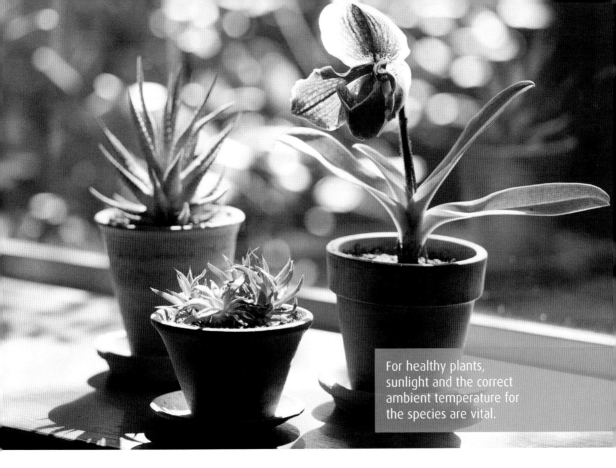

For healthy plants, sunlight and the correct ambient temperature for the species are vital.

LIGHT AND WARMTH

Sunlight is essential for plants to grow, and it must be in balance with temperature. In the wild, these are usually in harmony: as light intensity rises, so does the temperature. However, in homes—especially in winter—the temperature may be high but the light intensity low. Adjustments can be made to the temperature, but the temperature is usually selected to suit people rather than plants.

* The intensity of light varies from one season to another, as well as throughout the day. In the plant directory in Part Two (see pages 62–211), the amount of light needed in winter and summer is indicated for each plant.

* Light intensity rapidly decreases as distance from a window increases. The amount of illumination at 8ft (2.4m) from a window is 5–10% of that of the light reaching a windowsill.

* Temperatures vary throughout the year; those to suit plants in winter and summer are indicated in the individual listings in Part Two.

* In general, flowering houseplants need more light than those grown mainly for their foliage, while cacti require good light at all times.

- Plants should not be moved suddenly from dull light to strong light.
- Keep windows clean, especially during winter when light intensity is low. In summer, sheer curtains help to diffuse strong sunlight.
- Rooms decorated in light colors reflect more light than dark shades—a major benefit in winter.
- Leaves and stems soon turn toward the light source, causing distortion. Counteract this by turning plants a quarter of a turn every few days.
- In winter, plants close to windows may receive good light but be exposed to drafts from ill-fitting window frames, causing flower buds to fall off.

THE NEED FOR WATER

Like all living things, plants are mainly formed of water and, if deprived of it, eventually die. Some, such as cacti and other succulents, have water-storage mechanisms in their leaves and stems, but most plants need a regular supply. The amount required varies through the year and is influenced by light intensity and temperature.

Watering a Houseplant

There are several ways to water a houseplant. The usual method is "over the rim."

Water the compost and allow to drain.

This involves using an indoor watering can to pour water into the space between the top of the compost and the rim of the pot. Allow water to seep into the compost and drain through it into a saucer. After about 10 minutes, tip away excess water from the saucer.

Alternatively, where it is essential not to moisten the leaves (especially those that are hairy and soft, such as saintpaulias and *Episcia cupreata*), stand the pot in a bowl shallowly filled with water. When moisture rises to the compost's surface, remove the potted plant and allow excess water to drain.

HOW TO JUDGE IF A PLANT NEEDS WATER

More houseplants die each year from too little or too much water than for any other reason. Judging when to water is a skill derived from experience, although in recent years several specialized pieces of equipment have helped to take the guesswork out of this task. Year-round water requirements for individual types are indicated in the plant directory in Part Two. Here are several practical ways to judge if a plant needs water.

1. A handy "when to water" guide is that water is needed if the surface of compost in a pot has a light color. Conversely, when the compost is dark, it is probably sufficiently moist.

2. Place the clay pot on a flat surface and, without holding onto the pot, tap it with an empty sewing thread spool spiked on a bamboo cane. If this produces a ringing sound, the plant needs water; if the sound is dull and heavy, water is not required. (This technique does not work on plastic pots.)

3. It is possible to use a finger to test the compost's surface, but this eventually compacts the compost.

4. Moisture-indicating strips—sometimes known as watering signals—can be inserted and left in the compost to indicate the need for water.

5. Moisture meters (devices for assessing the moisture in compost) are accurate but involve inserting a spiked probe into the compost and getting a reading on a dial. Doing this repeatedly damages roots.

Dry compost is light in color.

Tap to check for dryness.

Gently feel the compost for moisture.

Moisture meters are accurate.

Saving a Plant with Exceptionally Dry Compost

Sometimes, compost becomes exceptionally dry, especially if watering is neglected in the summer or during vacations.

Place plants that do not like getting their leaves wet in a bowl of water to absorb water from below.

* If neglect is only superficial, stand the plant on a well-drained surface and water the compost two or three times. At each watering, the compost expands and makes it better able to retain moisture when more water is applied.

* If a plant is dramatically wilting, remove dead flowers and leaves and stand the plant in a bowl shallowly filled with water. When water seeps up to the surface of the compost, remove the plant and allow excess moisture to drain.

Rescuing a Plant with Wet Compost

In winter, when houseplants are usually not growing rapidly, plants are sometimes excessively watered, resulting in leaves and flowers wilting. If the compost is not totally saturated, there is a good chance of rescuing it.

With the plant still in its pot, support the compost with one hand and invert the plant and pot. Remove the pot. Use an absorbent cloth or disposable paper towel to soak up excess moisture—repeated wrappings are usually needed. Leave the root ball wrapped in absorbent paper until dry, but not bone-dry. If the root-ball is packed with roots that hold

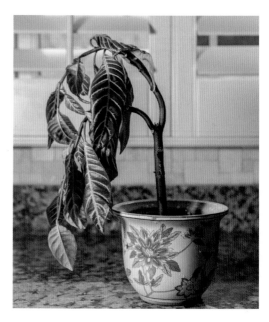

Wilting can be the result of excessive watering.

RESCUING AND REPOTTING
A PLANT
WITH WET COMPOST

1. Remove the pot.

2. Soak up excess moisture.

3. Wrap and leave to dry out.

4. Repot into a clean pot when the compost is only slightly moist.

Stand a plant with dry compost in a bowl of water.

it together, omit the wrapping. When the compost is only slightly moist, repot the root-ball into a clean pot.

Type of Water

Most houseplant enthusiasts use tap water, which suits the majority of plants. It is clean and readily available, and it is ideal as long as it is not too cold. However, houseplants such as azaleas dislike lime and grow best in slightly acidic soil. If the tap water is alkaline, boil it and allow it to stand until cool before use. Collecting defrosted iced water from a refrigerator and allowing it to reach room temperature is another option.

Rainwater is ideal, but ensure that it is clean and has not fallen on a dirt-contaminated roof or become stagnant in a barrel.

HUMIDITY AND MISTING

The amount of humidity in the air influences the health and growth of plants. Desert cacti and most other succulents survive in areas with little humidity, but plants native to forests usually need a humid atmosphere.

Signs of Excessive Humidity

1. Leaves and flowers that are tightly packed together sometimes become excessively damp.
2. Flower petals and buds eventually become covered in a furry mold.
3. Soft, hairy leaves become damaged before shiny, all-green ones do.
4. Cacti and other succulents develop patches of decay.
5. Plants with leaves that clasp stems become damaged; water becomes trapped at the junctions of leafstalks and leaves.

HOW TO CREATE HUMIDITY AROUND PLANTS

1. Stand plants in small groups to create a humid mini-environment.

2. Stand pots in trays with a 1in (25mm) layer of pebbles in the base, shallowly filled with water to just below the top of the pebbles. Moist air can then rise around the leaves.

3. Use a mist sprayer/mister, which is inexpensive, to coat the leaves in fine water droplets, but do not spray flowers or plants with hairy leaves.

4. Mist plants in the morning so moisture can evaporate before night. Dampness remaining on the leaves in late evening encourages the presence of diseases at night when the temperature falls.

5. Mist aerial roots, such as those on *Monstera deliciosa* and some Philodendrons, to help them to remain soft, pliable, and active.

6. Avoid spraying plants when they are in strong, direct sunlight; water droplets may act as lenses and burn the leaves.

7. Regular misting helps to discourage red spider mite infestation.

Signs of an Excessively Dry Atmosphere

1. Tips of leaves become curled, dry, and shriveled.
2. Flowers fade and become discolored, with flower buds eventually falling off.
3. Tips of shoots wilt and, later, shrivel.
4. Surfaces of leaves become dull.
5. The whole plant wilts if the temperature is high, with leaves eventually falling off.

REPOTTING HOUSEPLANTS

Eventually, most houseplants (except those grown for their short-term display) fill their pots with roots and need to be transferred to slightly larger ones. A plant left in the same pot will slowly deteriorate. When selecting a new pot, check the following.

* The new pot is clean, dry, and about 1in (25mm) larger. When a plant is already in a large pot, perhaps 6in (15cm) or more wide, the new pot can be 2in (5cm) larger.
* When repotting into a clay pot, put a piece of broken clay pot (known as a crock), concave side downward, in the base to prevent the drainage hole from

STEP-BY-STEP REPOTTING

1. The day before repotting, thoroughly water the compost and allow the excess to drain. This is essential since a plant with a dry root ball will not rapidly become established in a new pot.

2. Place the fingers of one hand over the top of the root ball and invert it, together with the pot. Sharply tap the rim on a hard surface (without damaging the plant's leaves), so the pot and root ball separate.

3. Fill a suitable pot with compost to about one-third of its depth and press to lightly pack it. (Add a crock in its base first if it is a clay pot.)

4. Without damaging the root ball, position it in the center of the pot. Check that the top of the root ball is about ½in (12mm) below the new pot's rim. Add or remove compost.

5. Keep the plant and root ball upright and carefully dribble fresh compost around it. Gently pack it until just covering the root ball. When repotting a plant in a large pot, leave a slightly larger space between the compost's surface and rim.

6. Stand the plant on a well-drained surface and gently water the compost from above, without unduly disturbing it. A couple of waterings may be necessary. Watering from above also helps to settle fresh compost around the root ball.

7. Stand the pot on a clean saucer or place it in a cachepot. Initially, position the plant in light shade for two to three days, or until established.

becoming blocked. This is unnecessary when repotting into plastic pots; these are usually filled with peat-based compost, which is more fibrous and less likely to fall out of the smaller drainage holes into the base.

* Use the same type of compost in which the plant is already growing.

FEEDING

To remain healthy, plants need a balanced diet throughout their lives. For most, this is provided by compost in a pot, with the addition of regular feeding or, for plants in large pots, top-dressing. Regular feeding makes a remarkable difference, and there are three main ways to do it.

Use a cachepot or place the pot on a saucer after repotting.

* **Liquid fertilizers** are the traditional, easiest, and most widely used choice for feeding houseplants. Concentrated fertilizers are diluted in clean water and applied to potting composts. First read the instructions and add the correct amount to clean water. Agitate and apply to moist compost. Many bromeliads have urns at their centers (resembling small vases formed by leaves); keep these topped up with water, and add weak liquid fertilizer, usually from spring to late summer.

Dilute liquid fertilizer in water and stir.

Apply liquid fertilizer to moist compost.

* **Fertilizer pills and sticks** are more recent innovations. They are pushed into the compost to provide food for several months. They are best used in spring and up to midsummer. If they are used in late summer, they provide food when some plants are resting. Unfortunately, unlike liquid feeding (which encourages the development of roots throughout the compost), pills and sticks concentrate nutrients in one position, resulting in an uneven spread of roots.

Insert a fertilizer stick into the compost.

* **Foliar feeds** are ideal for houseplants that can absorb nutrients through their leaves. Air plants are normally fed in this way. Plants rapidly respond to foliar feeding, and the technique is best used as a tonic for plants with smooth, non-hairy leaves. Avoid spraying flowers or using foliar feeds when plants are in strong sunlight. Strong foliar feeds will burn the leaves.

Remember that not all houseplants need feeding at the same frequency throughout the year. While most are fed during summer, not all need feeding in winter (see the plant directory in Part Two for details). Before feeding a plant, check that the compost is moist; this decreases the risk of roots becoming burned by

To prevent fertilizer from going all over the place when you foliar feed plants, simply place the plants in a plastic bag.

TOP-DRESSING LARGE HOUSEPLANTS

Instead of being repotted, large plants are usually top-dressed.

1. Use a small trowel to carefully remove the surface compost without damaging the roots. The depth of the compost that is removed is usually no more than 1in (25mm).

2. Add slow-release fertilizer to fresh compost and use it to top up the pot so its surface is about ½in (12mm) below the rim. Then, carefully water the compost using a watering can with a rose.

strong chemicals and helps spread plant foods throughout the compost.

Feeds that are too strong soon damage roots, so it is essential to adhere to the manufacturer's instructions. To avoid root damage, it is better to provide a plant with a weak liquid fertilizer than one that is too strong.

Add weak liquid fertilizer to a bromeliad's central urn.

GROOMING AND SUPPORTING

Grooming keeps houseplants attractive throughout their lives. Flowering houseplants need to have dead flowers removed, while others need to be supported or have their leaves cleaned. When removing dead flowers and leaves, put them into a bag and throw them away; do not scatter them around a plant, because decaying pieces of plants are unsightly and encourage the presence of diseases.

Wipe the leaf with a damp cloth to restore shine and remove dust.

Cleaning Leaves

Houseplants with large leaves, such as the Rubber Plant (*Ficus elastica*), benefit from having them cleaned. Dust and dirt left on leaves impairs their appearance and prevents sunlight from activating growth processes.

* Use a soft, damp cloth to clean large, shiny leaves. Support the leaf with one hand and carefully wipe the surface. To avoid burning, never do this when the plant is in strong sunlight.
* If a plant has a large number of small, shiny leaves, gently swirl them in a bowl filled with slightly warm water. When clean, remove the plant and stand it away from direct sunlight until dry, or it might burn.
* Use a soft brush to gently remove dust from hairy leaves. Blowing on leaves while brushing them helps to remove dust.

Swirl leaves under water to rinse off dust and dirt.

Tidying Stems and Shoots

* Some plants become untidy and benefit from having stems and shoots removed.

Use a paintbrush to clean dust off hairy leaves.

Trim off untidy long growth with a sharp pair of scissors.

For houseplants with long flower stems, break off from the base of the stem to discourage disease.

Snap off dead flowers between your thumb and forefinger.

Where a stem or shoot spoils a plant's symmetry, use sharp scissors to cut it back to just above a leaf-joint. Avoid leaving small stubs, which are unsightly and will die back.

* Young foliage plants often need to have a shoot tip removed to encourage bushiness. Use sharp scissors to cut back the stem to a leaf-joint, or hold the shoot between your fingers and snap it sideways.

* Some variegated plants occasionally produce all-green stems; cut these off.

Removing Dead Flowers

Dead flowers are unsightly and encourage the presence of diseases if left on a plant. Most dead flowers are removed by pinching them off between a finger and thumb. For houseplants such as cyclamen, remove the complete flower stem and dead flower; leaving short pieces of stem encourages the presence of diseases. Gently tug the stem so it parts from the plant's base.

Staking and Supporting

When plants need to be supported, it is essential that this is unobtrusive, whether you use traditional materials (raffia, green string, and

Form a hoop with pliable cane and attach the plant with string.

split canes) or more recent introductions (plastic frameworks and metal rings).

* Most houseplants need little support, but if it becomes necessary, use a thin split cane and soft green string. First tie the string to the support, then loop it around the stem just below a leaf-joint. Metal plant rings can also be used.

* Some climbing plants, such as *Jasminum polyanthum* (Pink Jasmine), benefit from a supporting hoop formed of pliable canes. When the plant is young and has shoots about 12in (30cm) long, insert pliable canes into the compost and train the stems around the canes.

* Climbing plants with aerial roots benefit from being given a moss pole as support (this is a stiff stake covered with several layers of moss). Use spirals of green string to hold it in position. Tie the plant's stems to the pole and keep the moss damp.

A moss pole works well as a support for a climbing plant with aerial roots.

VACATION CARE

Invariably, there are times when plants are left unattended for several days. This is not a problem in winter, when most are not very active, but arrangements need to be made to look after them in summer.

HELPING PLANTS SURVIVE

1. If you are going away for only a few days, place a plastic sheet on the floor in the center of a room and stand your plants on it. Fill their saucers with water.

2. Keep small plants moist by standing them in a shallow tray packed with moist peat.

3. Place a piece of capillary matting on a draining board and trail the other end into a sink full of water. Stand plants directly on it, not in their saucers. This works well for plants growing in peat-based compost in plastic pots, without crocks in their base.

4. Use wicks to keep compost moist in small pots. Push a wick into the compost and trail the other end into a pot filled with water.

5. Shallowly fill a wide basin with clean water and place one or more plants in it. This is ideal for houseplants that like plenty of moisture, such as some ferns.

6. Fill a shallow container with expanded, light-weight clay particles (which resemble small, hard, ceramic, shell-like pebbles with porous cores), add water to just below their surface, and stand plants on top.

Stand plants on capillary matting.

Use wicks to water plants.

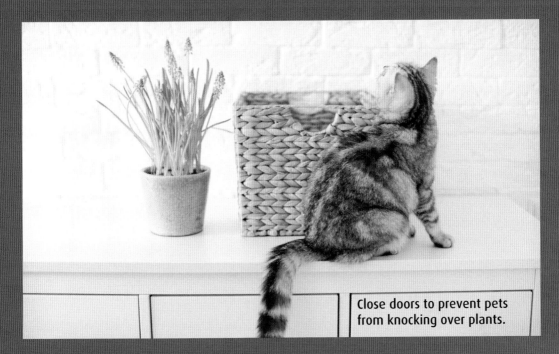

Close doors to prevent pets from knocking over plants.

BEFORE LEAVING HOME

1. Close the door of the room to prevent drafts from drying plants or from pets from knocking them over.
2. Draw the curtains in summer, especially those that face strong, direct sunlight.
3. A week before leaving home, check that plants are not infested with pests and diseases. Spray immediately if they are.
4. Remove faded flowers and those that will be past their prime by the time you return. Remove dead leaves.

Stand plants in a bowl of water.

Remove faded flowers.

Remove dead leaves.

HOUSEPLANT PROBLEMS

Few plants can escape from pests and diseases or cultural problems (often known as physiological disorders), such as leaves and flower buds falling off. It is much easier to prevent attack by pests and diseases than to eliminate them from badly affected plants. Here are some prevention tips.

* Buy plants from reputable sources.
* Inspect plants before buying.
* Regularly check for infestations.
* Never use garden soil instead of potting compost as it may contain weed seeds, pests, or diseases.
* Avoid leaving dead flowers and leaves around plants.
* Check root balls for soil pests when plants are being repotted.
* Never use infected plants as propagation material.

The chemicals permitted by legislation vary from country to country and state to state, so if prevention fails, check with your local nursery or garden center about the most suitable insecticide to use for your specific problem.

Pests

Aphids: also known as greenfly, aphis, and aphides, they are the main pests of houseplants. These small, usually green, sap-sucking insects infest flowers, shoot tips, and soft leaves, sucking sap and causing mottling and distortion. They also excrete honeydew, which attracts ants and encourages the presence of a fungal disease called sooty mold.

Control: spray with a suitable insecticide as soon as aphids are seen. Repeat every 10–14 days throughout summer.

Cyclamen mites: these infest a wide range of plants, including cyclamen, pelargoniums, saintpaulias (African Violets) and impatiens (Busy Lizzies). They are minute, eight-legged, spider-like creatures that cluster on the undersides of leaves. They suck sap, causing leaves to crinkle and darken. Flowering is shortened and buds become distorted and may fall off.

Control: remove and burn seriously infested leaves and flowers. Spray with an acaricide. Destroy badly infected plants to prevent the mites from spreading.

Mealy bugs: white, waxy, woodlice-like creatures that live in groups and especially infest ferns, palms, azaleas, and hippeastrums. They suck sap, causing distortion, loss of vigor, and yellowing of leaves. They excrete honeydew, which encourages the presence of ants and sooty mold.

Control: wipe off light infestations with cotton swabs dipped into methylated spirits (rubbing alcohol). Spray with a suitable insecticide or burn seriously infected plants.

Red spider mites: also known as greenhouse red spider mites, they are spider-like, minute, usually red, and have eight legs. They suck leaves, causing mottling and, if the infestation is severe, webs. These are unsightly, reduce air circulation around the plant, and make eradication difficult.

Control: mist-spray daily with clean water (but avoid spraying flowers or soft leaves) and spray with a suitable acaricide.

Scale insects: swollen, waxy-brown discs, usually static, under which female scale insects produce their young.

Control: young scale insects can be wiped away with a cotton swab dipped in methylated spirits (rubbing alcohol). Established colonies are difficult to eradicate, and badly contaminated plants are best burned.

Thrips: these tiny, dark brown, fly-like insects jump from one plant to another. They pierce leaves and flowers, sucking sap and causing silvery mottling and streaking. Undersides of leaves develop small globules of a red liquid that eventually turns black.

Control: spray several times with a suitable insecticide or burn seriously infected plants. Keep the compost moist, because dryness intensifies the damage caused by these insects.

Vine weevils: serious pests in the adult form, when young, and as larvae. Adults are beetle-like, with a short snout. They chew all parts of plants. The larvae—fat, legless, and creamy white, with brown heads—inhabit compost and chew roots.

Control: immediately water the compost with suitable insecticide and spray the leaves. Destroy badly infected plants.

Whitefly: small, moth-like white insects that flutter from one plant to another when disturbed. They have a mealy or powder-like covering and are mostly found on the undersides of leaves, sucking sap, causing distortion, and excreting honeydew, which encourages the presence of ants and sooty mold.

Control: eradication is not easy; several sprayings at five-day intervals with a suitable insecticide are essential.

Diseases

Black leg: a disease mainly of cuttings, especially of pelargoniums; the bases become black and soft.

Control: this is encouraged by cold, wet, airless compost, so ensure compost is well aerated when taking cuttings. If cuttings are infected, they are best removed and destroyed; for rare or unusual varieties, remove cuttings, cut off the blackened area, and reinsert the base in fresh compost.

Botrytis: also known as gray mold, it attacks soft parts of plants, such as flowers, shoots, and young leaves, covering them with a gray, furry mold.

Control: cut off and destroy infected parts. Spray infected plants with a suitable fungicide. Remove dead flowers to discourage spreading. Avoid damp, still air and excessive water.

Damping off: attacks seedlings soon after they germinate, causing them to turn black and collapse.

Control: sow seeds thinly in well-drained compost and place in a warm and well-aerated location. Avoid excessively watering the compost.

NONCHEMICAL CONTROL OF PESTS AND DISEASES

Apart from growing plants healthily, with adequate moisture, food, and circulation of air, there are other ways to keep them healthy and to ward off pests and diseases.

1. Mist plants with clean water where there is a risk (or presence) of red spider mites.

2. Regularly remove dead leaves and flowers.

3. Use insecticidal soaps, which are ideal against a wide range of insects and mites.

4. Investigate biological controls, which means using other insects and mites to control pests. These are especially suitable where insects have developed resistance to chemical controls. Biological controls exist for aphids, caterpillars, mealy bugs, soft scale insects, red spider mites, thrips, vine weevil larvae, and whiteflies. Ask your garden center for advice.

Powdery mildew: fungal disease that produces a white, powdery coating. It usually appears in spring and summer, infecting leaves, flowers, and stems.

Control: remove badly infected leaves, stems, and flowers; increase ventilation and keep the atmosphere dry.

Rusts: complex diseases that are more problematic in sunrooms and conservatories than indoors. They produce raised rings of brown or black spots. Plants become unsightly and lose their vigor.

Control: remove and burn infected plants and increase ventilation. Do not propagate from infected plants.

Sooty mold: black, fungal disease that grows on leaves, stems, and flowers covered with honeydew (see aphids and other sap-sucking insects on page 34). At first it appears in small clusters, but later covers the entire surface.

Control: spray with a suitable insecticide against sap-sucking insects. Use a damp cloth to remove the black growth from leaves. Flowers are best cut off.

Viruses: microscopic particles that invade plants (and animals), causing disorders in the tissue but seldom killing the host immediately.

Control: regularly spray with a suitable insecticide against sap-sucking insects (which probably introduced the problem to your plants) and burn badly infected plants.

Cultural Problems

Also known as physiological disorders, these are not caused by pests or diseases but by environmental problems.

Wilting: there are several causes, including too much water, too little water, and the result of soil pests that eat and destroy roots. Usually, plants wilt because they are short of water; if the compost is dry, water the plant several times. Alternatively, stand the plant, in its pot, in a bowl of water. Later, remove and allow excess water to drain. If a plant wilts and the compost is exceptionally wet, remove the pot and dry the root-ball (see page 21).

Leaves fall off: occasionally, leaves fall off as a result of factors such as dry or wet soil, pests and disease, and cultural influences, including a sudden drop in temperature. Reposition the plant and keep it in an even, warm temperature away from drafts. Leaves that become yellow and gradually drop off are the result of excessive watering or inadequate feeding.

Flower buds fall off: this may happen if the plant is in a draft or a dry atmosphere or has received a sudden chill. Buds often drop off if a plant is severely knocked.

Damaged leaf surfaces: lack of water may make the edges of leaves become crisp and brown, but straw-colored patches on leaves, especially soft and hairy ones, are the result of water splashing on the surface, which is then burnt by strong sunlight.

APPLYING CHEMICALS

There are several ways in which insecticides and fungicides can be applied to plants.

1. **Spraying** is the most common method. One way to treat a plant in a small house or apartment is to put it in a large plastic bag, which can be temporarily sealed after spraying is complete.

2. **Dusting** is popular, and a puffer-type applicator is readily available.

3. **Insecticidal sticks** can be pushed into the compost. The plant's roots absorb the chemical and the whole plant becomes toxic to insects.

SAFETY TIPS

1. Follow the manufacturer's instructions and never use stronger or weaker solutions.

2. Unless recommended, never mix two different chemicals.

3. Check that the chemical is suitable for the plants being sprayed—some plants are susceptible to specific chemicals.

4. Store chemicals away from children and household pets.

5. Avoid spraying if animals are in the room; fish and birds are especially harmed by chemical sprays.

6. Never allow children or animals to lick or chew plants that have been sprayed.

7. Only apply chemicals suitable for use indoors. This will be indicated on the label, but if in doubt, ask your nursery or garden center for advice.

INCREASING
HOUSEPLANTS

There are several easy ways to increase your houseplants and, for a few of them, very little equipment is needed. Some methods produce many new plants, while in others just one new plant is created, such as when air layering a *Ficus elastica* (Rubber Plant).

SOWING SEEDS

Many houseplants can be increased from seeds. If you want several plants of the same type, this is a relatively inexpensive method. Bear in mind, though, that equipment such as seed trays, pots, and compost are needed, as well as a greenhouse, sunroom, or conservatory where gentle warmth can be provided.

Step-by-Step: Sowing Seeds

1. If only a few seeds are to be sown, use a small, shallow pot, but a plastic seed tray is better for larger numbers. Fill it with seed compost and use your fingers to pack it, especially around the edges.

2. Place more compost in the seed tray and use a straight-edged piece of wood to level it with the rim. Then, use a flat-surfaced piece of wood to pack the compost to ½in (12mm) below the rim so the seeds can be lightly covered and watered without water spilling out.

3. Tip a few seeds into a piece of light-colored, stiff paper folded into a V-shape. Then gently tap its end to distribute seeds evenly over the surface, but not within ½in (12mm) of the edges.

4. Use a flat-based horticultural sieve to cover the seeds in seed compost to about three times their thickness. Alternatively, use a culinary sieve.

5. Shallowly fill a bowl with clean water and stand the seed tray in it until moisture seeps to the surface. Remove and allow excess water to drain.

6. Cover the seed tray with a clear plastic lid to prevent the compost's surface from drying out and to help maintain a somewhat warm temperature. Wipe the inside of the cover every day to remove condensation. Remove it entirely when seedlings germinate and small seed leaves can be seen.

SOWING SEEDS

HOUSEPLANTS RAISED FROM SEEDS

Many houseplants can be raised from seeds—from foliage and flowering plants to palms, cacti, and other succulents. The following are just a few popular examples of seed-raised plants, but there are many others.

FLOWERING HOUSEPLANTS

Begonia semperflorens (Wax Begonia)

Calceolaria x herbeohybrida (Slipper Plant)

Cyclamen persicum (Cyclamen)

Exacum affine (Persian Violet)

Impatiens walleriana (Busy Lizzie)

Kalanchoe blossfeldiana (Flaming Katy)

Primula malacoides (Fairy Primrose)

Schizanthus pinnatus (Butterfly Flower)

Senecio cruentus (Cineraria)

FOLIAGE HOUSEPLANTS

Coleus blumei (Flame Nettle)—now botanically *Solenostemon scutellarioides* and earlier *Plectranthus scutellarioides*, it is still known and sold as Coleus

Grevillea robusta (Silky Oak)

PALMS FOR THE HOME

Chamaedorea elegans (Parlour Palm)

Chamaedorea seifrizii (Reed Palm)

Howea forsteriana (Kentia Palm)

TAKING CUTTINGS

Many houseplants can be increased from cuttings. There are several different types of cuttings, but most important is that they should be healthy and free from pests and diseases.

Step-by-Step: Stem-Tip Cuttings

Each cutting is formed of a piece of stem, several leaves, and a terminal shoot. They are usually 3–4in (7.5–10cm) long and, if possible, taken from the outer parts of a mother plant, where they have received good light and are growing healthily and robustly.

1. Use a sharp knife to sever a healthy shoot close to the parent plant (do not leave a short stub).
2. Also use a sharp, clean knife to prepare the cutting, slicing just below a leaf-joint. Then cut off the lower leaves.
3. Fill a small pot with equal parts moist peat and sharp sand and pack it to ½in (12mm) below the rim. Use a small dibber to form a hole into which the stem can be inserted about 1in (25mm) deep. Pack the compost around the stem and lightly water from above.
4. Insert 3–4 short split canes into the compost and cover with a plastic bag. Use an elastic band to secure the bag around the pot. When shoots develop, remove the bag. Later, when growing robustly, transfer the rooted cutting to another pot.

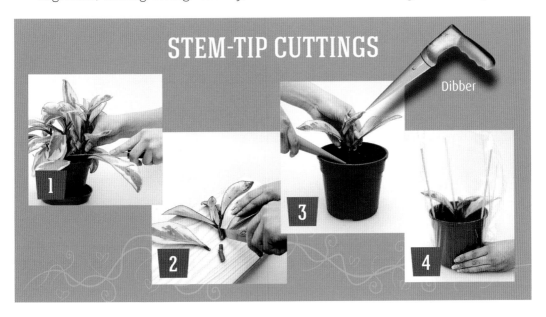

STEM-TIP CUTTINGS

Dibber

1

2

3

4

Step-by-Step: Leaf-Stem Cuttings

Leaf-stem cuttings resemble stem-tip cuttings, but without the tip. This is an excellent way to increase plants with long, trailing stems that have leaves at regular intervals. Examples include both variegated and all-green forms of *Hedera helix* (Common Ivy).

1. Select a long, healthy stem from a mother plant and sever it just above a leaf. Do not use old, hard stems.
2. Cut the stem to form several cuttings; cut just above a leaf so that each cutting is formed of a leaf and piece of stem about 1 ½in (36mm) long. The stem part can be shortened if it is too long.
3. Fill a pot with equal parts moist peat and sharp sand and pack to ½in (12mm) below the rim. Use a dibber to insert 3–4 cuttings in each pot, each ¾—1in (18–25mm) deep, spaced out but not less than ½in (12mm) from the pot's side. Pack compost around their bases and gently water from above.
4. Insert 3–4 short split canes into the compost and cover with a plastic bag secured around the pot with an elastic band. When shoots develop, remove the bag. Cuttings can be separated and repotted individually, but to produce a display more quickly just repot the entire pot of cuttings into another pot.

LEAF-STEM CUTTINGS

LEAF-PETIOLE CUTTINGS

Step-by-Step: Leaf-Petiole Cuttings

Often used to increase *Saintpaulia ionantha* (African Violet), this involves cuttings formed of a leaf and a small stalk (petiole).

1. Form each cutting by severing the stem of a healthy leaf at the base of a mother plant, but avoid leaving short spurs or stems.
2. Use a sharp knife to trim back stems to about 1 ½in (36mm) long.
3. Fill a small pot with equal parts moist peat and sharp sand; pack to ½in (12mm) below the rim. Dip the end of each cutting in hormone rooting powder and use a small dibber to insert it so the base of the leaf is just above the compost. Pack compost around the stem and lightly water from above. Several cuttings can be inserted in each pot and transferred to individual pots when they develop small shoots.

Step-by-Step: Whole-Leaf Cuttings

Large-leaved begonias, such as *Begonia rex* (Rex Begonia) and *Begonia masoniana* (Iron Cross Begonia), can be increased by this method or the one following (leaf-square cuttings).

1. The day before taking cuttings, water the mother plant so the leaves are full of moisture. Select a healthy leaf and sever its stem just above the plant's base.
2. Invert the leaf and use a sharp knife to sever the stem close to the underside of the leaf.

WHOLE-LEAF CUTTINGS

3. Cut across the main veins on the leaf's underside with a sharp knife, positioning cuts ¾–1in (18–25mm) apart. Do not cut completely through the leaf.
4. Fill a seed tray with equal amounts moist peat and sharp sand; pack it to ½in (12mm) below the rim. Place the leaf on the compost vein-side downward and lightly press it down, holding in position with a few pebbles (or use U-shaped pieces of wire).
5. Put a plastic cover over the seed tray and place in gentle warmth. Keep the compost lightly moist.
6. Later, when small plants develop from the leaf's surface, these can be moved to individual pots.

Step-by-Step: Leaf-Square Cuttings
1. Cut a healthy leaf from a parent plant and sever the stem close to the leaf's underside. Position the leaf upside down and cut it into 1 ¼in (3cm) square pieces. Each must have several veins.
2. Fill a seed tray with equal parts moist peat and sharp sand; pack to ½in (12mm) below the rim. For each leaf cutting, use the blade of a knife to form a slit about ½in (12mm) deep in the compost's surface. Push the side of a cutting (which was

nearest to the leafstalk) into the slit and pack compost around it.

3. Insert other leaf cuttings—not within ½in (12mm) of the edge—and gently water from above without disturbing the cuttings. Allow excess moisture to drain, then cover with a plastic dome.

4. When young shoots develop from each cutting, transfer them to individual pots.

Step-by-Step: Leaf-Triangle Cuttings

This is another popular way to increase large-leaved houseplants. As with leaf-square cuttings, several new plants can be produced from one leaf.

1. Cut a healthy leaf from a parent plant and sever the stem close to the leaf's underside. Leave the leaf upside down and cut it into triangles, which tend to be longer than the squares of leaf-square cuttings (see page 48). These can be inserted deeper into the compost, which helps to give them greater stability.

LEAF-SQUARE CUTTINGS

LEAF-TRIANGLE CUTTINGS

2. Fill a seed tray with equal parts moist peat and sharp sand; pack to ½in (12mm) below the rim. Use a knife to form a slit ¾–1in (18–25mm) deep in the compost's surface. Push the end of a cutting (which was nearest to the leafstalk) into the slit and pack compost around it.
3. Insert other leaf cuttings (not within ½in [12mm] of the side) and gently water from above without disturbing the cuttings. Allow excess moisture to drain, then cover with a plastic dome.
4. When young shoots develop from each cutting, transfer them to individual pots.

Step-by-Step: Cross-Leaf Cuttings

Sometimes known as cross-section and leaf-section cuttings, this technique is often used to increase *Streptocarpus x hybridus* (Cape Primrose).

1. The day before taking cuttings, water the mother plant and allow excess water to drain. Sever a healthy leaf close to the base, place on a board, and cut into cross-sections 2in (5cm) wide.
2. Fill a seed tray with equal parts moist peat and sharp sand; pack to ½in (12mm) below the rim. With a sharp knife, form slits ¾in (18mm) deep. Insert the cutting's base into the slit. Pack compost around it.
3. Gently water the compost. Allow the leaf's surface to dry and place a transparent lid on top. When young shoots develop from the leaf, detach them individually (usually with part of the parent leaf still attached) and transfer them to a small pot. Small but established cuttings have a better chance of being repotted successfully than large ones.

CROSS-LEAF CUTTINGS

HORIZONTAL CANE CUTTINGS

Step-by-Step: Horizontal Cane Cuttings

Several thick-stemmed houseplants can be increased in this way, including *dieffenbachias* (Dumb Cane), *dracaenas*, and *cordylines*.

1. Water the mother plant the day before taking cuttings. Sever a strong, healthy stem at its base, trying not to spoil the plant's shape.
2. Use a sharp knife to cut the stem into 2–3in (5–7.5cm) long pieces; each part must have at least one strong bud (they grow from leaf-joints).
3. Fill a 5in (13cm)-wide pot with equal parts moist peat and sharp sand; pack to ½in (12mm) below the rim. Press each cutting horizontally into the compost to half its thickness, with the strongest bud facing upward. Hold in place with pieces of U-shaped wire.
4. Lightly water the compost, allow excess to drain, and cover with a plastic lid. When shoots and roots develop, transfer them to individual pots.

Step-by-Step: Vertical Cane Cuttings

Several houseplants can be increased in this way, including yuccas and *dracaenas*. Sometimes these cuttings are known as Ti-log cuttings (a word of Polynesian derivation), although properly this name refers solely to *Cordyline fruticosa*, earlier known as *Cordyline terminalis* and *Dracaena terminalis*. These Ti-logs are widely sold

VERTICAL CANE CUTTINGS

as specially prepared cuttings, with their ends covered in wax. The following advice refers specifically to them.

1. Cut off the wax from the lower end, but leave the wax covering the top intact, as this prevents loss of moisture before the cutting forms roots.
2. Add a handful of equal parts moist peat and sharp sand to the base of a pot. Hold the cutting with the waxed end upward and pot it up so its base is 1 ½–2in (36–50mm) deep. Gently water the compost.
3. To encourage rapid rooting, put the pot and cutting in an opaque bag and place in gentle warmth. Check the compost every 10 days to ensure it is still damp. When shoots appear, remove the bag and slowly acclimatize the plant to a lower temperature. Later, usually in 2–4 weeks, transfer the rooted cutting to a larger pot.

Step-by-Step: Cactus Cuttings

Some cacti, especially those that form clusters, can be increased from cuttings taken in spring or early summer. Remember to wear gloves when taking these cuttings.

1. Use a sharp knife to sever a few stems from the plant's base, taking care not to spoil its shape. Allow cut ends to dry for a day or so, then insert in compost.
2. Fill a small pot with equal parts moist peat and sharp sand; pack to ½in (12mm) below the rim. Use a small dibber to form a hole to a depth about one-

third of the cutting's length. Insert the cutting, pack the compost, and lightly water from above. When young shoots develop or fresh growth develops at the cutting's top, transfer to an individual pot.

Step-by-Step: Small-Leaved Succulent Cuttings

Several succulents, such as *echeverias* and *crassulas*, have small leaves that can be removed and encouraged to develop roots.

1. Water the mother plant the day before taking cuttings. Select a healthy leaf and gently snap it off downward or sideways. Take several cuttings without spoiling the plant's shape. Allow cut edges to dry for a day or so.

2. Fill a pot with equal parts moist peat and sharp sand; pack to ½in (12mm) below the rim. Add a dusting of sharp sand to the surface. Use a small dibber or knife to insert each cutting to about one-third of its length.

3. When young shoots and roots develop from a cutting's base, it can be transferred to another pot.

CACTUS CUTTINGS

1

2

SMALL-LEAVED SUCCULENT CUTTINGS

1

2

3

Dividing

Dividing is a quick and easy way to increase houseplants with fibrous roots and several stems. Spring and early summer are the best times to divide them.

Step-by-Step: Dividing

1. The day before dividing a congested plant, water the compost, and allow excess to drain. Then, to divide, place a hand over the soil-ball and invert the pot. Sharply tap the pot's rim on a hard surface so the pot and root ball separate.
2. Place the root ball on a firm surface and gently tease it apart into several substantial-sized pieces, making certain that each part has healthy roots, stems, and leaves.
3. Prepare a clean, dry pot, filling its base with compost. Position one of the new plants centrally in the pot, so that the base of the stems is about ½in (12mm) below the rim. Dribble compost around the roots, packing it in layers until ½in (12mm) below the rim. Tap the side of the rim to level the compost.
4. Water the plant from above by using a watering can with a fine rose. This helps to settle the compost around the roots of the newly divided plants. Place the plant in a location with light shade until it is established. By dividing a congested plant, several new plants can be produced.

DIVIDING

HOUSEPLANTS SUITABLE FOR DIVIDING

Aspidistra elatior (Aspidistra)

Goeppertia makoyana (Peacock Plant, previously known as *Calathea makoyana* and *Maranta makoyana*) and other *calatheas*

Chlorophytum comosum (Spider Plant)

Ctenanthe oppenheimiana tricolor (Never-Never Plant)

Cyperus alternifolius (Umbrella Grass)

Ferns (many can be divided)

Fittonia argyroneura (Silver Net Plant) and other *fittonias*

Maranta leuconeura (Prayer Plant) and other *marantas*

Saintpaulia ionantha (African Violet)

Sansevieria trifasciata var. laurentii (Mother-in-Law's Tongue)

Soleirolia soleirolii (Mind Your Own Business)

Spathiphyllum wallisii (Peace Lily)

LAYERING

This is an easy way to increase houseplants with pliable stems, such as those that trail or climb. Late spring and early summer are the best times to do this.

Step-by-Step: Layering

1. The day before layering a plant, water the compost to ensure stems are turgid. Allow excess moisture to drain. Fill a clean pot, packing moist peat and sharp sand to about ½in (12mm) below the rim.
2. Bend a long stem near a leafstalk and about 5in (13cm) from its end. This bend is not meant to sever the stem, but to constrict it so roots will develop at that point.
3. Use a small piece of U-shaped wire to secure the bent section of stem 1–1 ½in (25–36mm) deep in the compost. Pack the compost around and over the stem and lightly water it.
4. Put the mother plant and the layered stem in a plastic tray so that they can be moved together. When fresh shoots develop, use a sharp knife to sever the stem.

LAYERING

HOUSEPLANTS SUITABLE FOR LAYERING

Epipremnum aureum (Devil's Ivy)

Hedera canariensis 'Variegata' (Canary Island Ivy, also sold as *Hedera algeriensis* 'Gloire de Marengo'). There are many other variegated forms that can be propagated in the same way.

Hedera helix (Common Ivy): there are many variegated forms

Philodendron scandens (Sweetheart Plant)

Air Layering

Air layering is used to increase large, woody houseplants such as *Ficus elastica* (Rubber Plant) that have grown tall, with bare woody stems. Best undertaken in early and midsummer, it involves partially severing a stem just below the lowest leaf and encouraging it to develop roots.

Step-by-Step: Air Layering a Rubber Plant

1. Choose a healthy plant that is bare of leaves on the lower part of its stem. The top 1 ½ft (45cm) of the plant should have healthy leaves.
2. Use a sharp knife to make an upward-slanting cut, two-thirds through the stem and 3–4in (7.5–10cm) below the lowest leaf. Take care that the top part does not snap off.
3. Insert a matchstick into the cut to hold it open. Trim off its ends and use a small brush to coat the cut surfaces with a hormone rooting powder.
4. Wind a piece of clear polythene film, about 9in (23cm) wide and 12in (30cm) long, around the stem, and secure its base about 2in (5cm) below the cut.
5. Fill the tube formed by the polythene with moist peat. Pack it to about 3in (7.5cm) below the tube's top. Tie the top around the stem with string.

AIR LAYERING A RUBBER PLANT

6. Keep the compost in the pot moist so the plant continues to grow. Six to eight weeks later you will see through the polythene that roots have formed.

7. Hold the top of the plant and sever the stem directly below the polythene. Carefully remove the film.

8. Immediately place the plant into potting compost in a clean pot. Dribble compost around the roots and carefully pack it. Support the stem until the plant is established. Do not throw away the old plant. Instead, cut it to about 9in

HOUSEPLANTS SUITABLE FOR AIR LAYERING

Dieffenbachia (Dumb Cane)
Ficus elastica (Rubber Plant)
Monstera deliciosa (Swiss Cheese Plant)

(23cm) high and place in gentle warmth, about 54–64°F (12–18°C). Young shoots will develop from the stem to form a multistemmed plant.

HOUSEPLANTS FROM PLANTLETS

A few houseplants develop small plantlets along or at the edges of leaves; these can be removed and encouraged to produce roots and develop into separate plants.

Step-by-Step: Plants with Plantlets

1. Choose a healthy mother plant (such as the *Kalanchoe daigremontiana* shown on page 60) and gently detach plantlets growing along a leaf's edges.
2. Fill a pot that is 3in (7.5cm) wide with compost and pack it to about ½in (12mm) below the rim. Space out plantlets on the surface and slightly press them into the compost. Gently water the plantlets from above, taking care not to disturb them.
3. When rooted and growing well, transfer them to individual small pots. When potting rooted plantlets of *Kalanchoe delagoensis*, put three plants in each pot.

PLANTS WITH PLANTLETS

HOUSEPLANTS FROM RUNNERS

Some houseplants produce plantlets at the ends of long, runner-like stems, perhaps the best-known example being *Chlorophytum comosum* (Spider Plant). Although this can be performed throughout the year, late spring to late summer is best.

Step-by-Step: Increasing a Spider Plant

1. Water the compost in the mother plant and select several long, healthy stems, each with a healthy plantlet at its end. Fill several pots with compost and pack it to ½in (12mm) below the rim. Position a plantlet in the compost and use U-shaped pieces of wire to hold it in place. Lightly water the compost and stand the mother plant and the pots with pegged-down plantlets in a large seed tray. This makes it easy to move them as a unit.

2. When new shoots develop from the plantlet, sever the runner close to the plantlet. Also cut off the stem close to the mother plant's base.

OTHER HOUSEPLANTS WITH RUNNERS AND PLANTLETS

Kalanchoe daigremontiana (Mexican Hat)
Kalanchoe delagoensis (Chandelier Plant)
Saxifraga stolonifera (Mother of Thousands)
Saxifraga stolonifera 'Tricolor' (Magic Carpet)

INCREASING A SPIDER PLANT

Part Two
PLANT DIRECTORY

FOLIAGE PLANTS

FOLIAGE HOUSEPLANTS ARE POPULAR, CREATING COLOR AND INTEREST OVER A LONG PERIOD, WITH ONLY OLD AGE OR NEGLECT SPOILING THEIR DISPLAY AND SHORTENING LIFE EXPECTANCY. MANY PLANTS, SUCH AS VARIEGATED IVIES AND ASPIDISTRAS, HAVE LONG BEEN LIVING FEATURES IN HOMES. OTHERS ARE LESS HARDY, BUT WELL WORTH GROWING.

Chinese Evergreen
Aglaonema commutatum

Evergreen perennial with lance-shaped, dark-green leaves up to 5in (13cm) long and 2in (5cm) wide, and having silvery-gray zones on either side of the lateral veins. During midsummer it produces white spathes (arum-type flowers), 2in (5cm) long, followed by dark red berries. There are several forms, including "Golden Evergreen" (*Aglaonema commutatum* 'Pseudobracteatum,' sometimes sold as *Aglaonema pseudobracteatum*), with rich green, spear-shaped leaves and creamy-gold markings.

↕ **Height:** 6–8in (15–20cm)

↔ **Spread:** 9–12in (23–30cm)

❄ **Winter:** 50–61°F (10–16°C). Direct light without full sun

☀ **Summer:** 61–75°F (16–24°C). Indirect light

❤ **Care:** In winter, keep compost evenly moist; in summer, water more freely and feed every 3–4 weeks. Repot in spring, usually every 3–4 years.

✿ **Propagation:** Divide congested plants when being repotted. Until established, place in 50–61°F (10–16°C).

Crystal Anthurium
Anthurium crystallinum

Evergreen perennial with heart-shaped leaves, up to 2ft (60cm) long and 1ft (30cm) wide. They are violet when young, maturing to deep green, with veins and mid-ribs on the upper surfaces lined in ivory; pale pink beneath.

↕ **Height:** 15–18in (38–45cm)

↔ **Spread:** 12–15in (30–38cm)

❄ **Winter:** 55–61°F (13–16°C). Indirect light

☀ **Summer:** 61–70°F (16–21°C). Light shade

❤ **Care:** In winter, keep compost barely moist; in summer, water freely but ensure good drainage, and feed every 2–3 weeks with weak liquid fertilizer. Repot in spring when roots fill the pot, usually every 2–3 years.

✿ **Propagation:** Divide congested plants in spring, ensuring each new plant has a growing point. Alternatively, sow seeds in late spring or early summer; place in 75°F (24°C).

Saffron Spike, Zebra Plant
Aphelandra squarrosa

Evergreen shrub with lance-shaped, dark-green leaves, up to 9in (23cm) long, and veins heavily lined in ivory. Yellow, cone-shaped flower heads, 3–4in (7.5–10cm) long, appear from mid- to late summer. 'Louisae' has yellow flowers streaked red and slightly narrower leaves, with bold white markings along the veins. Other forms include 'Brockfeld' (crinkle-edged leaves with ivory lines), 'Dania' (compact, with white veins), and 'Leopoldii' (pale yellow flowers and dark-green leaves with white veins).

↕ **Height:** 1–2ft (30–60cm)

↔ **Spread:** 12–15in (30–38cm)

❄ **Winter:** 50–55°F (10–13°C). Full sun or direct light without full sun

☀ **Summer:** 55–64°F (13–18°C). Direct light without full sun

❤ **Care:** In winter, keep compost barely moist, and feed at 3-week intervals if the plant is actively growing; in summer, keep it moist but not waterlogged, and feed every 2 weeks. Repot in spring, usually every year.

✿ **Propagation:** Take 3–4in (7.5–10cm)-long cuttings during spring and early summer; place in 70°F (21°C).

Foxtail Fern, Plume Asparagus

Asparagus densiflorus 'Myersii'

Sometimes known as *Asparagus densiflorus* 'Meyeri,' this fern-like, evergreen perennial initially has an upright nature, then arches, with stiff, spire-like stems packed with bright green, needle-like leaves.

‡ **Height:** 12–18in (30–45cm)

↔ **Spread:** 1 ½–2 ½ft (45–75cm)

❊ **Winter:** 50–55°F (10–13°C). Direct light without full sun

❋ **Summer:** 50–61°F (10–16°C). Indirect light or light shade

♥ **Care:** In winter, keep compost only slightly moist; water freely in summer and feed every 2 weeks with weak liquid fertilizer. Repot in spring when roots fill the pot, usually every 1–2 years.

✿ **Propagation:** Divide congested plants in spring or early summer. Until established, place in 50–55°F (10–13°C).

Asparagus Fern, Emerald Feather, Emerald Fern, Sprengeri Asparagus, Sprenger's Asparagus

Asparagus densiflorus 'Sprengeri'

Earlier known as *Asparagus sprengeri*, this arching, sprawling, semiprostrate evergreen perennial has wiry, trailing stems with bright green, needle-like leaves. 'Compactus' is the dwarf version and less trailing.

‡ **Height:** 10–12in (25–30cm)

↔ **Spread:** 2 ½–3ft (75–90cm), sometimes more

❊ **Winter:** 45–50°F (7–10°C). Direct light without full sun

❋ **Summer:** 50–61°F (10–16°C). Indirect light or light shade

♥ **Care:** In winter, keep compost only slightly moist; water more freely in summer and feed every 2 weeks with weak liquid fertilizer. Repot in spring when roots fill the pot, usually every 1–2 years.

✿ **Propagation:** Divide congested plants in spring or early summer. Until established, place in 50°F (10°C).

Asparagus Fern, Fern Asparagus, Florist Fern, Lace Fern
Asparagus setaceus

Earlier known as *Asparagus plumosus*, this evergreen perennial is really a climbing plant, but in its juvenile, non-climbing stage is an ideal houseplant, with mid-green, lace-like leaves borne in horizontal tiers.

⭥ **Height:** 15–18in (38–45cm) in its juvenile form

↔ **Spread:** 15–24in (38–60cm) in its juvenile form

❋ **Winter:** 41–45°F (5–7°C). Direct light without full sun

❋ **Summer:** 45–55°F (7–13°C). Indirect light or light shade

❤ **Care:** In winter, keep compost only slightly moist; in summer, water more freely and feed every 2–3 weeks with weak liquid fertilizer. Repot in spring when roots fill the pot, usually every 1–2 years.

✿ **Propagation:** Divide congested plants in spring or early summer. Until established, place in 45°F (7°C).

Barroom Plant, Cast Iron Plant, Iron Plant, Parlor Plant
Aspidistra elatior

Earlier known as *Aspidistra lurida*, this evergreen perennial has glossy, dark-green, oblong to lance-shaped leaves, up to 20in (50cm) long. The variegated form (*Aspidistra elatior* 'Variegata') has green leaves with whitish-cream stripes.

⭥ **Height:** 12–15in (30–38cm)

↔ **Spread:** 1 ½–2ft (45–60cm)

❋ **Winter:** 45–50°F (7–10°C). Direct light without full sun

❋ **Summer:** 50–59°F (10–15°C). Indirect light or light shade

❤ **Care:** In winter, keep compost slightly moist; in summer, water freely and feed every 3–4 weeks. Repot in spring when roots fill the pot, usually every 2–3 years.

✿ **Propagation:** Divide congested plants in spring or early summer, when being repotted. Until established, place in 50°F (10°C).

Eyelash Begonia
Begonia bowerae

Earlier known as *Begonia boweri*, this small-leaved begonia has irregularly triangular, green leaves that are about 3in (7.5cm) long; they are peppered with chocolate-brown spots. From late winter to late spring, it produces pale pink or white flowers. Begonia 'Tiger' (shown here) is a hybrid of *Begonia bowerae* and is sometimes sold as *Begonia bowerae* 'Tiger.'

↕ **Height:** 6–10in (15–25cm)

↔ **Spread:** 6–10in (15–25cm)

❉ **Winter:** 55°F (13°C). Direct light without full sun

✹ **Summer:** 55–61°F (13–16°C). Indirect light

❤ **Care:** In winter, keep compost just moist; in summer, water freely and feed every 2 weeks. Repot in spring when roots fill the pot, often every year when the plant is young.

✿ **Propagation:** Divide congested plants in spring. Until established, place in 55°F (13°C).

Iron Cross Begonia
Begonia masoniana

Rhizomatous-rooted begonia with large, lopsided, slightly heart-shaped green leaves with corrugated surfaces, distinctively patterned with 4–5 deep bronze-purple bars radiating from the center. It occasionally produces small, greenish-white flowers during spring and summer.

↕ **Height:** 8–10in (20–25cm)

↔ **Spread:** 10–12in (25–30cm)

❉ **Winter:** 55–59°F (13–15°C). Direct light without full sun

✹ **Summer:** 55–68°F (13–20°C). Indirect light

❤ **Care:** In winter, keep compost barely moist, allowing it to dry slightly between waterings; in summer, water freely without continually saturating the compost, and feed every 2–3 weeks. Repot in spring when roots fill the pot, usually every year when young.

✿ **Propagation:** Divide congested plants in spring, when being repotted. Alternatively, take leaf cuttings in late spring or early summer and place in 55–61°F (13–16°C).

King Begonia, Painted-Leaf Begonia, Rex Begonia
Begonia rex

This rhizomatous-rooted perennial has large, slightly heart-shaped, lopsided, wrinkle-surfaced, dark-green leaves with silvery zones near their edges. It is rarely grown: it is mainly the related plants, known as Rex Hybrids, that are seen. The hybrid forms have colorful leaves, up to 10in (25cm) long, that create dominant displays. Many named forms exist.

↕ **Height:** 9–12in (23–30cm)

↔ **Spread:** 12–15in (30–38cm)

❄ **Winter:** 55–59°F (13–15°C). Direct light without full sun

↔ **Spread:** 55–64°F (13–18°C). Indirect light

❤ **Care:** In winter, keep compost barely moist, allowing it to dry slightly between waterings; in summer, water freely without continually saturating the compost, and feed every 2–3 weeks. Repot in spring when roots fill the pot, usually every year when young.

✿ **Propagation:** Divide congested plants in spring, when being repotted, or take leaf cuttings in late spring or early summer. Cut leaves into squares or triangles and place in 55–61°F (13–16°C).

Brain Plant, Cathedral Plant, Cathedral Windows, Peacock Plant
Calathea makoyana

Now botanically known as *Goeppertia makoyana* and earlier as *Maranta makoyana*, this beautiful evergreen perennial has oval silvery-green leaves, 6in (15cm) long, with mid-green edges irregularly marked by dark-green splashes. The undersides have reddish-purple splashes.

↕ **Height:** 15–18in (38–45cm)

↔ **Spread:** 15–18in (38–45cm)

❄ **Winter:** 55–61°F (13–16°C). Direct light without full sun

☀ **Summer:** 61–70°F (16–21°C). Indirect light or light shade

❤ **Care:** In winter, keep compost evenly moist; in summer, water freely and feed every 2 weeks. Repot in spring when roots fill the pot, usually every year when young.

✿ **Propagation:** Divide congested plants in spring. Until established, place in 55–61°F (13–16°C).

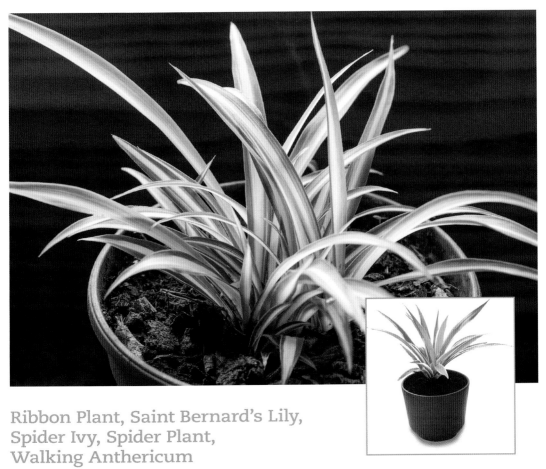

Ribbon Plant, Saint Bernard's Lily, Spider Ivy, Spider Plant, Walking Anthericum

Chlorophytum comosum

Evergreen perennial with long, narrow green leaves striped white. There are several attractive cultivars, including 'Variegatum' (green leaves edged white or cream), 'Vittatum' (central white strip, green edges), and 'Mandanum' (earlier listed as 'Mandaianum,' with a central yellow stripe and green edges). Plants develop long, stiff but flexible stems with small plantlets at their ends.

↕ **Height:** 8–10in (20–25cm), then cascading and trailing

↔ **Spread:** 15–24in (38–60cm)

❄ **Winter:** 45–50°F (7–10°C). Direct light without full sun

☀ **Summer:** 50–64°F (10–18°C). Indirect light, or direct light without full sun

♥ **Care:** In winter, keep compost barely moist but not dry; in summer, water freely but ensure good drainage and feed every 10–14 days. Repot in spring when roots fill the pot, every year when young and, later, every other year. When congested, roots swell and push the plant out of the pot, making watering difficult.

✿ **Propagation:** Divide congested plants when being repotted. Also, peg down plantlets into compost. Place in 50–55°F (10–13°C) until established and showing signs of growth.

Kangaroo Vine
Cissus antarctica

Vigorous evergreen perennial climber that develops
glossy, heart-shaped, and pointed dark-green leaves,
about 4in (10cm) long and 2in (5cm) wide, with
scalloped and spiny edges.

‡ **Height:** 6–8ft (1.8–2.4m) when in a pot

↔ **Spread:** 2–3ft (60–90cm) when in a pot

❄ **Winter:** 45–50°F (7–10°C). Direct light without
   full sun

✳ **Summer:** 50–64°F (10–18°C). Indirect light or
   light shade

❤ **Care:** In winter, keep compost just moist; in summer, water freely and feed every 2–3 weeks. Repot in
   spring when roots fill the pot, usually every 1–2 years.

✿ **Propagation:** Take 3–4in (7.5–10cm)-long cuttings from side-shoots during midsummer and place in 61°F
   (16°C).

Grape Ivy, Natal Vine, Venezuela Treebine
Cissus rhombifolia

Earlier known as *Rhoicissus rhomboidea*, this will
climb and spread to 20ft (6m) in a greenhouse or
conservatory. Dark-green leaves are each formed of
3 diamond-shaped, scalloped, spiny-edged leaflets.
The form 'Ellen Danica,' known as the Mermaid Vine
(pictured), is not as vigorous as the species; it is ideal
for growing in a pot indoors.

‡ **Height:** 4–6ft (1.2–1.8m) in a pot indoors

↔ **Spread:** 1–1 ½ft (30–45cm) in a pot indoors

❄ **Winter:** 45–50°F (7–10°C). Full sun

✳ **Summer:** 50–61°F (10–16°C). Light shade

❤ **Care:** In winter, keep compost just moist; in summer, water freely and feed every 2–3 weeks. Repot in
   spring when roots fill the pot, usually every 1–2 years.

✿ **Propagation:** Take 3–4in (7.5–10cm) cuttings from side-shoots during midsummer and place in
   61°F (16°C).

Croton, Joseph's Coat, Variegated Laurel
Codiaeum variegatum var. *pictum*

Evergreen perennial with a range of dazzling colors on leathery leaves that vary in shape and pattern. In greenhouses, these plants reach 8–10ft (2.4–3m) high, but are superb for decorating homes when young and in small pots. The range includes 'Bravo' (green splashed with yellow), 'Carrierei' (yellow-green leaves maturing to reveal red centers), 'Disraeli' (slender mid-green leaves blotched creamy yellow), and 'Mrs. Iceton' (oval, black-green leaves marked between the veins with red and pink).

↕ **Height:** 1 ½–2ft (45–60cm) range

↔ **Spread:** 1–1 ½ft (30–45cm) range

❄ **Winter:** 55–59°F (13–15°C). Full sun, or direct light without full sun

☀ **Summer:** 59–64°F (15–18°C). Direct light without full sun

❤ **Care:** In winter, keep compost barely moist; in summer, water more freely but ensure compost is well drained, and feed every 2–3 weeks. Repot in spring when roots fill the pot, usually every year when young.

✿ **Propagation:** Take 3in (7.5cm) cuttings during spring or early summer. Place in 75°F (24°C).

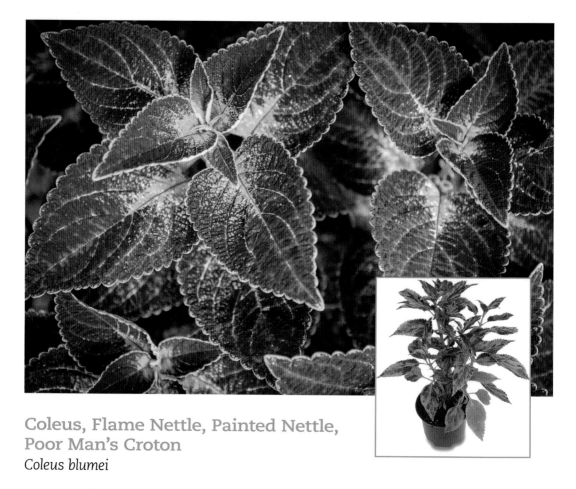

Coleus, Flame Nettle, Painted Nettle, Poor Man's Croton
Coleus blumei

Now botanically known as *Solenostemon scutellarioides* and earlier as *Plectranthus scutellarioides,* it is still known and sold as Coleus. It is a popular plant with richly colored, nettle-like leaves in brilliant shades of red, maroon, yellow, and green. They have scalloped or saw-toothed edges. Tubular blue and white flowers appear during late summer and into autumn, but are best nipped off to prevent them from detracting from the beauty of the leaves. There is a wide range of named hybrids, most with a bushy nature, but some trailing. They can be overwintered in warm rooms or heated greenhouses and conservatories, but are best discarded in early winter and replaced by fresh plants in early summer.

↕ **Height:** 15–18in (38–45cm)

↔ **Spread:** 12–15in (30–38cm)

❄ **Winter:** 55°F (13°C) if overwintered. Full sun, or direct light without full sun

☀ **Summer:** 50–59°F (10–15°C). Full sun, but shade from strong midday sunlight

❤ **Care:** In winter, keep overwintered plants barely moist; in summer, water freely and feed every 2–3 weeks. Repot young plants in spring.

✿ **Propagation:** From mid-spring to late summer, take stem-tip cuttings, 3–4in (7.5–10cm) long, and place in 61–64°F (16–18°C). Repot into individual pots when rooted. They can also be raised from seeds.

Flaming Dragon, Good Luck Plant, Hawaiian Good Luck Plant, Polynesian Ti, Red Dracaena, Ti Log, Ti Plant, Tree of Kings
Cordyline fruticosa

Earlier known as *Cordyline terminalis* and *Dracaena terminalis*, this evergreen has lance-shaped, mid- to deep-green leaves flushed with red, purple, or cream. Cultivars include 'Guilfoylei' (leaves striped red and pink or white), 'Red edge' (green, streaked red), and 'Tricolor' (red and purple).

‡ **Height:** 1 ½–3ft (45–90cm) in an indoor pot

↔ **Spread:** 15–18in (38–45cm) in an indoor pot

❄ **Winter:** 50–55°F (10–13°C). Direct light without full sun

☀ **Summer:** 55–75°F (13–24°C). Direct light without full sun, or light shade

❤ **Care:** In winter, keep compost lightly moist; in summer, water more freely and feed every 2 weeks. Repot in spring when roots fill the pot, usually every 2–3 years.

✿ **Propagation:** During midsummer, cut up the stems of old and leggy plants into 3in (7.5cm) pieces. Insert them in equal parts moist peat and sharp sand and place in 64–70°F (18–21°C).

Never-Never Plant
Ctenanthe oppenheimiana

Evergreen perennial with a bushy nature and lance-shaped, leathery green leaves with silvery-gray feathering above and purple to wine-red below. Leaves are borne on long stalks. It is usually grown in the form 'Tricolor,' with a velvety surface and cream-colored blotches between leaves and reddish-purple beneath.

‡ **Height:** 8–12in (20–30cm)

↔ **Spread:** 10–15in (25–38cm)

❄ **Winter:** 61°F (16°C). Direct light without full sun

☀ **Summer:** 61–70°F (16–21°C). Direct light without full sun, or indirect light

❤ **Care:** In winter, keep compost evenly moist; in summer, water more freely and feed every 2–3 weeks. Repot in spring when roots fill the pot, usually every 2 years.

✿ **Propagation:** Divide congested plants in spring and place in 61–64°F (16–18°C) until established.

Dumb Cane, Leopard Lily, Spotted Dog Cane
Dieffenbachia maculata

Also known as *Dieffenbachia picta*, this evergreen perennial has oblong leaves, up to 12in (30cm) long, in various colors. It gains the name Dumb Cane from the sap, which causes loss of speech for a short while after contact with the mouth. Also avoid getting sap in your eyes. There are many cultivars, including 'Exotica' (leaves suffused yellow and green) and 'Rudolph Roehrs' (pale yellow, with some veins in ivory).

↕ Height: 1 ½–4ft (45cm–1.2m)

↔ Spread: 1–1 ½ft (30–45cm)

❄ Winter: 59–64°F (15–18°C). Full sun, or direct light without full sun

✹ Summer: 64–75°F (18–24°C). Indirect light or light shade

❤ Care: In winter, keep compost evenly but barely moist; in summer, water freely but ensure good drainage, and feed every 2–3 weeks. Repot in spring when roots fill the pot, usually every 2–3 years.

✿ Propagation: In spring, cut bare stems into 2–3in (5–7.5cm) pieces, peg them horizontally onto compost and place in 70–75°F (21–24°C).

Aralia Ivy, Botanical Wonder, Fat-Headed Lizzie, Ivy Tree, Miracle Plant, Tree Ivy
X *Fatshedera lizei*

Evergreen shrub-like climber with 5-lobed green leaves. When young, it has a single stem, but develops further stems with age, then sprawls and climbs. It can be kept bushy by pinching out the growing tips to encourage further side-shoots to develop. 'Variegata' has leaves with creamy white blotches and edges, and is less vigorous than the all-green type.

↕ Height: 4–6ft (1.2–1.8m)

↔ Spread: 2–3ft (60–90cm)

❄ Winter: 39–45°F (4–7°C). Direct light without full sun, or indirect light

✹ Summer: 50–64°F (10–18°C); avoid high temperatures. Indirect light or light shade

❤ Care: In winter, keep compost barely moist, but give more water if the temperature rises; in summer, water freely and feed every 2–3 weeks. Repot in spring when roots fill the pot, usually every year.

✿ Propagation: From late spring to midsummer, take 4–5in (10–13cm) cuttings. Place in 61°F (16°C).

False Castor Oil Plant, Formosa Rice Tree, Glossy-Leaved Paper Plant, Japanese Fatsia, Paper Plant
Fatsia japonica

Often erroneously known as the Castor Oil Plant (*Ricinus communis*), this moderately hardy, shrub-like plant has large, palm-like, rich glossy-green leaves with 7–9 coarsely tooth-edged lobes. Clusters of rounded white flowers appear only occasionally on houseplants. 'Variegata' has white tips and edges to its leaves.

↕ **Height:** 3–5ft (90cm–1.5m) indoors or in a conservatory

↔ **Spread:** 2 ½–4ft (75cm–1.2m) indoors or in a conservatory

❄ **Winter:** 37–45°F (3–7°C); avoid high temperatures. Direct light without full sun

☀ **Summer:** 50–64°F (10–18°C); avoid high temperatures. Indirect to bright light, without full sun

❤ **Care:** In winter, keep compost just moist; in summer, water more freely and feed every 2–3 weeks. Repot in spring, usually every year when young.

❀ **Propagation:** When repotting, remove and repot sucker-like shoots from around its base and place in 45–50°F (7–10°C) until rooted.

Benjamin Fig Tree, Benjamin Tree, Java Fig, Small-Leaved Rubber Plant, Tropical Laurel, Weeping Fig
Ficus benjamina

Graceful, evergreen shrub or tree with slightly pendulous branches bearing stiff leaves, light green at first, darkening later. There are several superb forms with narrow or variegated leaves.

↕ **Height:** 4–6ft (1.2–1.8m) or more

↔ **Spread:** 3–4ft (90cm–1.2m) or more

❄ **Winter:** 55–61°F (13–16°C). Direct light without full sun

☀ **Summer:** Avoid excessively high temperatures, i.e., above 75°F (24°C). Direct light without full sun, or indirect light

❤ **Care:** In winter, keep compost lightly moist; in summer, water more freely and feed every 2–3 weeks. Repot in spring when roots fill the pot, usually every 2 years. Top-dress large plants.

❀ **Propagation:** Take 2–4in (5–10cm) cuttings during late spring and early summer. Place in 61–64°F (16–18°C).

Assam Rubber, India Rubber Fig, India Rubber Plant, Rambong-Rubber, Rubber Plant, Snake Tree
Ficus elastica

Widely grown houseplant with a single stem and stiff, glossy leaves. There are many forms, including 'Decora' (dark, large leaves), 'Doescheri' (pink-tinted, pale-green leaves with ivory edges), 'Schrijveriana' (variegated cream patches), 'Tricolor' (cream variegations, sometimes flushed pink), and 'Black Prince' (near-black foliage).

↕ **Height:** 3–5ft (90cm–1.5m) when young

↔ **Spread:** 1 ½–2ft (45–60cm) when young

❄ **Winter:** 61–64°F (16–18°C). Direct light without full sun

☀ **Summer:** 61–75°F (16–24°C). Indirect light, or direct light without full sun

♥ **Care:** In winter, keep compost lightly moist; in summer, water more freely and feed every 2–3 weeks. Repot in spring when roots fill the pot, usually every 2 years. When plants are large, top-dress the compost instead of repotting.

✿ **Propagation:** Take 4–6in (10–15cm) cuttings during late spring and early summer. Place them in 70–75°F (21–24°C). Alternatively, use air layering (see pages 57–59) for large plants with bare stems in early and midsummer.

Climbing Fig, Climbing Rubber Plant, Creeping Fig, Creeping Rubber Plant
Ficus pumila

Earlier known as a *Ficus repens*, this evergreen has a climbing, trailing nature and heart-shaped, dark-green leaves. Attractive cultivars include 'Minima' (small leaves, compact), 'Sonny' (variegated leaves with white edges), and 'Variegata' (leaves lined and marbled in cream and green).

↕ **Height:** 4–5ft (1.2–1.5m), more when grown as a climber

↔ **Spread:** 4–5ft (1.2–1.5m), more when grown as a climber

❄ **Winter:** 45–50°F (7–10°C). Direct light without full sun

☀ **Summer:** 50–61°F (10–16°C). Indirect light or light shade

♥ **Care:** In winter, keep compost lightly moist; in summer, water freely and feed every 2 weeks. Repot in spring when roots fill the pot, usually every 2 years.

✿ **Propagation:** Take 2–4in (5–10cm)-long cuttings during spring and early summer. Place in 64°F (18°C).

Variegated Canary Island Ivy
Hedera canariensis 'Gloire de Marengo'

Earlier known as *Hedera canariensis* 'Variegata' and currently as *Hedera algeriensis* 'Gloire de Marengo,' this hardy, resilient evergreen climber has large, slightly lobed green leaves with dominant silvery-gray centers, merging to white at the edges.

- ↕ **Height:** 5–8ft (1.5–2.4m) in an indoor pot
- ↔ **Spread:** Climber
- ❄ **Winter:** 35–45°F (2–7°C); avoid high temperatures. Direct light without full sun, or indirect light
- ☀ **Summer:** 45–50°F (7–10°C); avoid high temperatures. Indirect light
- ❤ **Care:** In winter, keep compost lightly moist; in summer, water freely and feed every 2–3 weeks. Repot in spring when roots fill the pot, usually every 3 years. Top-dress large plants.
- ✿ **Propagation:** Take 3–4in (7.5–10cm) stem cuttings or tip cuttings in midsummer. Place in 59–64°F (15–18°C).

Common Ivy, English Ivy
Hedera helix

Evergreen climber with a variable nature. Young plants have smaller and more lobed leaves than old ones. The range of cultivars used as houseplants is wide, including all-green types and variegated types (see sidebar).

↕ **Height:** 1 ½–3ft (45–90cm) when indoors

❀ **Winter:** 41–50°F (5–10°C). Full sun, or direct light without full sun

↔ **Spread:** Climbing and trailing

❋ **Summer:** 50–61°F (10–16°C). Indirect light or light shade

❤ **Care:** In winter, keep compost lightly moist; in summer, water more freely and feed every 2–3 weeks. Repot in spring when roots fill the pot, usually every 3 years. Top-dress large plants.

✿ **Propagation:** Take 3in (7.5cm) stem cuttings in summer. Place in 59–64°F (15–18°C).

Baby's Tears, Dot Plant, Flamingo Plant, Freckle Face, Measles Plant, Pink Dot, Pink Polka, Polka Dot Plant
Hypoestes phyllostachya

Earlier known as *Hypoestes sanguinolenta,* this bushy, sprawling, evergreen perennial produces a mass of oval, olive-green, spear-tipped leaves covered with white to pinkish spots and blotches. Superb cultivars include 'Bettina' (lighter-colored markings), 'Carmina' (bright red leaves), 'Purpuriana' (plum-colored markings), and 'Wit' (leaves marbled white).

↕ **Height:** 1 ½–2ft (45–60cm)

❀ **Winter:** 50–55°F (10–13°C). Direct light without full sun

↔ **Spread:** 1 ½–2ft (45–60cm)

❋ **Summer:** 55–68°F (13–20°C). Indirect light

❤ **Care:** In winter, keep compost lightly moist; in summer, water more freely and feed every 2–3 weeks. Repot in spring when roots fill the pot, usually every year when young.

✿ **Propagation:** Take 3in (7.5cm) stem-tip cuttings in late spring and early summer. Place in 70°F (21°C).

HEDERA HELIX CULTIVARS

SMALL, ALL-GREEN LEAVES

'Annette' (also known as 'California'): matte-green, 5-lobed leaves

'Chicago': 5-lobed leaves

'Green Ripple': usually 3-lobed leaves with distinctive and attractive veins

'Parsley Crested' (often sold as *Hedera helix cristata* and widely known as Parsley Ivy): 5-lobed leaves with wavy edges

'Pittsburgh': robust nature, 5-lobed leaves

VARIEGATED LEAVES

'Eva': leaves variegated cream and green

'Glacier': long a popular houseplant ivy; 3 distinctive lobes variegated silvery-gray, with creamy white edges

'Harald': leaves variegated 2-tone green and cream

'Jubilee': dark-green leaves with golden centers

'Kolibri': leaves variegated green and white

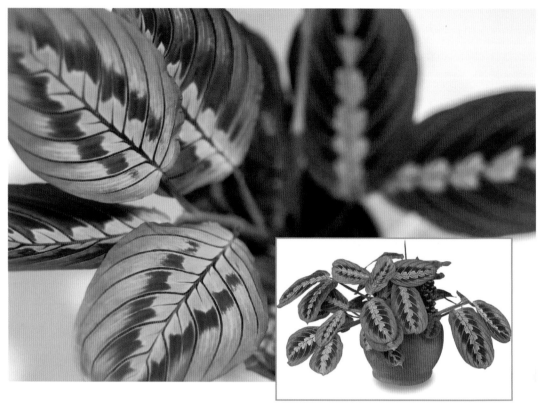

Prayer Plant, Ten Commandments
Maranta leuconeura

Evergreen perennial with beautiful leaves that close in the evening and are held erect, as if in prayer. Young leaves have an emerald-green background, with brown-purple blotches between the veins. The undersides are gray-green, shot with purple. There are several forms, including *Maranta leuconeura* 'Kerchoveana' (*Maranta kerchoveana*), widely known as Rabbit's Tracts or Rabbit's Foot (descriptive of the leaves). At first, the leaves are emerald-green with red blotches between the main veins, but with age become dark green with maroon blotches. *Maranta leuconeura* 'Erythrophylla' (Herringbone Plant)—also known as *Maranta leuconeura tricolor*, *Maranta erythrophylla*, and *Maranta leuconera* 'Erthyroneura'—has leaves with a deep olive-green background, grayish-green edges, vivid red veins, and bright green, irregular-edged markings along the midrib.

↕ **Height:** 6–8in (15–20cm)

↔ **Spread:** 10–12in (25–30cm)

❋ **Winter:** 55–61°F (13–16°C). Direct light without full sun

☀ **Summer:** 61–64°F (16–18°C). Indirect light or light shade

❤ **Care:** In winter, keep compost lightly moist; in summer, water more freely and feed every 2–3 weeks. Repot in spring when roots fill the pot, usually every year when young.

✿ **Propagation:** Divide congested plants when being repotted and place in 61°F (16°C) until established.

Breadfruit Vine, Ceriman, Cheese Plant, Cut-Leaf Philodendron, Fruit Salad Plant, Hurricane Plant, Mexican Breadfruit, Monstera, Split-Leaf Philodendron, Swiss Cheese Plant, Window Plant

Monstera deliciosa

Evergreen perennial with a climbing, sprawling nature. Dark-green leaves can be 3 ½ft (1m) long and 1 ½–2ft (45–60cm) wide. Indoors, leaves are smaller, deeply notched, and perforated. Mature plants have creamy yellow spathes up to 6in (15cm) long, followed by club-shaped fruits. 'Variegata' has marbled leaves streaked with cream and yellow.

‡ **Height:** 6–12ft (1.8–3.6m), sometimes more

↔ **Spread:** 3–5ft (90cm–1.5m)

❋ **Winter:** 45–50°F (7–10°C). Full sun

✸ **Summer:** 50–70°F (10–21°C). Direct light without full sun, or indirect light

❤ **Care:** In winter, keep compost moist; in summer, water more freely but allow to become slightly dry between waterings. Feed every 2–3 weeks in summer, avoiding strong concentrations, which damage roots. Repot in spring when roots fill the pot, usually every year when young. Later, just top-dress the compost.

❀ **Propagation:** During early summer, cut off the growing tip, together with a mature leaf and an aerial root, if possible. Insert the cutting in equal parts moist peat and sharp sand and place in 75–80°F (24–27°C).

Jaburan Lily, Jaburan Lilyturf, Snakebeard, White Lily, White Lilytuft

Ophiopogon jaburan

Evergreen perennial with stiff but arching, narrow, grass-like, all-green leaves. Variegated forms are more usually grown, including 'Vittatus' (sometimes known as 'Variegatus'), 'Argenteo-vittatus,' and 'Aureo-variegatus,' all with yellow- or white-striped leaves.

‡ **Height:** 10–15in (25–38cm)

↔ **Spread:** 10–15in (25–38cm)

❋ **Winter:** 41–50°F (5–10°C). Direct light without full sun, or full sun

✸ **Summer:** 50–61°F (10–16°C). Direct light without full sun

❤ **Care:** In winter, keep compost evenly moist; in summer, water more freely and feed every 2–3 weeks. Repot in spring when roots fill the pot, often every year.

❀ **Propagation:** Divide congested plants when being repotted and place in 50°F (10°C) until established.

PELARGONIUM

A group of popular houseplants with a sub-shrubby nature, Pelargoniums are often confusingly called geraniums because their leaf shapes resemble those of the garden geranium (a herbaceous perennial totally unrelated to pelargoniums). Several types of pelargoniums are used to decorate homes, some with superb flowers, others with attractive leaves. On the following pages are some with scented leaves.

↕ **Height:** See individual plants on pages 84–85	↔ **Spread:** See individual plants on pages 84–85
❄ **Winter:** In temperate climates, plants can be overwintered in a greenhouse or conservatory in 45–50°F (7–10°C). Direct light	✳ **Summer:** 55–61°F (13–16°C). Direct light, but provide light shade if the temperature rises dramatically
♥ **Care:** In winter, keep compost barely moist, but water more freely in summer.	
✿ **Propagation:** Take stem-tip cuttings, about 3in (7.5cm) long, in mid- and late summer. Insert in equal parts moist peat and sharp sand. Place in 55–61°F (13–16°C) on a greenhouse bench and cover initially with a couple of sheets of newspaper. When rooted, transfer the cuttings to individual pots.	

Rose Geranium, Rose-Scented Geranium
Pelargonium capitatum

Soft-stemmed plant with light-green, deeply lobed, velvety, somewhat crinkled leaves with a rose-like fragrance. It produces mauve-pink flowers with darker veins.

  ↕ **Height:** 12–18in (30–45cm)   ↔ **Spread:** 12–15in (30–38cm)

Lemon Geranium, Lemon-Scented Geranium
Pelargonium crispum

Slender shrub, with green, hoary, deeply lobed leaves with a distinctive lemon and balm fragrance when bruised. Rose-pink flowers appear in umbrella-like heads from early to late summer. Closely related Pelargonium crispum 'Minor' (Finger Bowl Pelargonium) has leaves with a sweet and citron-like fragrance.

  ↕ **Height:** 1 ½–2ft (45–60cm)   ↔ **Spread:** 15–18in (38–45cm)

Nutmeg Geranium
Pelargonium fragrans

Soft-stemmed shrub with gray-green, velvety, 3-lobed leaves with a nutmeg and pine redolence. The flowers are white and prominently spotted and veined in red.

  ↕ **Height:** 3–4ft (90cm–1.2m)   ↔ **Spread:** 1 ½–2ft (45–60cm)

Rose Geranium, Rose-Scented Geranium, Sweet-Scented Geranium

Pelargonium 'Graveolens'

Hoary, green, deeply lobed leaves reveal a sweet, rose-like fragrance when bruised. It produces rose-pink flowers with dark purple spots during mid- and late summer.

↕ **Height:** 2–2 ½ft (60–75cm)   ↔ **Spread:** 15–18in (38–45cm)

Apple-Scented Geranium
Pelargonium odoratissimum

Somewhat sprawling plant with light-green, velvety, round to heart-shaped leaves with a ripe-apple scent. Small, white flowers in summer.

↕ **Height:** 8–15in (20–38cm)   ↔ **Spread:** 1–2ft (30–60cm)

Almond-Scented Geranium, Almond-Scented Pelargonium, Oak-Leaved Geranium, Village Oak Geranium
Pelargonium quercifolium

Triangular to oblong, lobed and tooth-edged, mid-green leaves with the fragrance of almond combined with a hint of balsam. It has rose-colored flowers with deep purple veins during early and midsummer.

↕ **Height:** 2 ½–4ft (75cm–1.2m)   ↔ **Spread:** 1 ½–2ft (45–60cm)

Herb-Scented Geranium, Mint Geranium, Peppermint Geranium
Pelargonium tomentosum

Pale-green, soft, hairy leaves with dense, white downy-haired undersides and a distinctive, strong peppermint fragrance. White flowers peppered with red appear during summer.

↕ **Height:** 1–2ft (30–60cm)   ↔ **Spread:** 15–18in (38–45cm)

Emerald Ripple, Emerald-Ripple Peperomia, Green-Ripple Peperomia, Little Fantasy Peperomia
Peperomia caperata

Evergreen perennial with heart-shaped, glistening green leaves with a ripple-like surface. From spring to late autumn it bears white flowers in spikes up to 6in (15cm) high. Occasionally, they branch and have an antler-like nature.

⬍ **Height:** 4–8in (10–20cm) plus height of flowers

↔ **Spread:** 5–6in (13–15cm)

❄ **Winter:** 50–55°F (10–13°C). Direct light without full sun

☀ **Summer:** 55–64°F (13–18°C). Indirect light

❤ **Care:** In winter, keep compost barely moist; in summer, water thoroughly, allowing to dry slightly between waterings, and feed every 3–4 weeks. Repot in late spring, when roots fill the pot, usually every 2 years.

❀ **Propagation:** Take leaf-petiole (leaf and leafstalk) cuttings during summer. Place in 64°F (18°C).

Tree Philodendron
Philodendron bipinnatifidum

Evergreen perennial with glossy green leaves. Young leaves are heart-shaped; mature ones—up to 2ft (60cm) long and 1 ½ft (45cm) wide—are broadly 3-lobed and slowly develop deep incisions that may extend almost to the midrib.

⬍ **Height:** 3–4ft (90cm–1.2m)

↔ **Spread:** 3–3 ½ft (90cm–1m)

❄ **Winter:** 55–64°F (13–18°C); it can survive temperatures down to 50°F (10°C) for short periods. Direct light without full sun

☀ **Summer:** 64–75°F (18–24°C). Direct light without full sun, or indirect light

❤ **Care:** In winter, keep compost just moist; in summer, water more freely but ensure good drainage (continually wet compost damages roots). Feed every 3 weeks during summer. Repot in spring when roots fill the pot, usually every year when young. Later, top-dress the compost but avoid damaging surface roots.

❀ **Propagation:** Divide congested plants in early summer. Until established, place in 61–64°F (16–18°C).

Blushing Philodendron, Red-Leaf Philodendron
Philodendron erubescens

Vigorous evergreen climber with arrow-shaped leaves up to 12in (30cm) long and 7in (18cm) wide on mature plants, borne on long purple leafstalks. When young, leaves are rose-pink, slowly becoming dark, glossy green with a coppery tinge. There are several forms, including 'Red Emerald' (compact, with arrow-shaped leaves, pale bronze when young, becoming dark olive-green with narrow, purplish edges) and 'Burgundy' (young foliage is coppery-red, gradually becoming olive-green with burgundy undersides).

↕ **Height:** 4–6ft (1.2–1.8m)

↔ **Spread:** 15–18in (38–45cm)

❄ **Winter:** 55–64°F (13–18°C). Direct light without full sun

☀ **Summer:** 64–75°F (18–24°C). Direct light without full sun, or indirect light

❤ **Care:** In winter, keep compost barely moist; in summer, water freely but ensure good drainage, and feed every 3–4 weeks. Repot young plants annually in spring, and thereafter about every 2 years. When large, top-dress the compost. Provide a moss-covered pole for support.

❀ **Propagation:** Divide congested plants in early summer. Place in 61–64°F (16–18°C) until established.

Heartleaf Philodendron, Sweetheart Plant, Sweetheart Vine
Philodendron scandens

Moderately vigorous climbing evergreen perennial that forms a dense array of heart-shaped, mid-green leaves up to 4in (10cm) long and 3in (7.5cm) wide. When young, the leaves have an attractive bronze shade. The variegated form has cream blotches on the lower half of each leaf.

↕ **Height:** 3 ½–5ft (1–1.5m)

↔ **Spread:** 8–15in (20–38cm)

❄ **Winter:** 55–64°F (13–18°C). Direct light without full sun

☀ **Summer:** 64–75°F (18–24°C). Direct light without full sun, or indirect light

❤ **Care:** In winter, keep compost barely moist; in summer, water more freely and feed every 3 weeks. Repot in spring when roots fill the pot, usually every 2 years. Provide a moss-covered pole for support.

❀ **Propagation:** Take 4in (10cm) cuttings in early summer. Place in 70–75°F (21–24°C).

Aluminum Plant, Watermelon Pilea
Pilea cadierei

Evergreen perennial with leathery, oval, dark-green, slightly quilted leaves that have silvery splashes between the veins. The form 'Nana' is smaller, up to 9in (23cm) high. *Pilea* 'Bronze' is similar, with dull bronze-green leaves, 3in (7.5cm) long, and silvery marks between the veins.

‡ **Height:** 10–12in (25–30cm)

↔ **Spread:** 8–10in (20–25cm)

❄ **Winter:** 50–55°F (10–13°C). Direct light without full sun, or indirect light

☀ **Summer:** 61–75°F (16–24°C). Indirect light

♥ **Care:** In winter, keep compost barely moist; in summer, water more freely and feed every 2 weeks. Repot in spring when roots fill the pot, usually every year when young.

✿ **Propagation:** Take 3–4in (7.5–10cm) stem-tip cuttings in spring or early summer. Place in 64–70°F (18–21°C).

Friendship Plant, Panamica Panamiga, Pan-American Friendship Plant
Pilea involucrata 'Norfolk'

This bushy, slightly trailing evergreen perennial has oval to pear-shaped, silvery-gray leaves with bronze-green along the veins. If the plant is in shade, leaves are more green than bronze. The undersides are red.

‡ **Height:** 8–10in (20–25cm)

↔ **Spread:** 8–10in (20–25cm)

❄ **Winter:** 55–61°F (13–16°C). Indirect light or light shade

☀ **Summer:** 61–75°F (16–24°C). Light shade

♥ **Care:** In winter, keep the compost barely moist; in summer, water more freely and feed every 2 weeks. Repot in spring when roots fill the pot, usually every year when young.

✿ **Propagation:** Take 3in (7.5cm) stem-tip cuttings in spring and early summer. Place in 64–70°F (18–21°C).

Artillery Plant, Gunpowder Plant, Mossy Pilea
Pilea microphylla

Earlier known as *Pilea muscosa*, this evergreen perennial with small, mid-green leaves has a fern-like appearance. From late spring to late summer it produces small, greenish-yellow flowers that puff out clouds of pollen when disturbed, causing great amusement, especially to children.

↕ **Height:** 8–10in (20–25cm)

↔ **Spread:** 10–12in (25–30cm)

❋ **Winter:** 50–55°F (10–13°C). Direct light without full sun, or indirect light

✹ **Summer:** 61–75°F (16–24°C). Indirect light or light shade

❤ **Care:** In winter, keep compost lightly moist; in summer, water freely and feed every 2–3 weeks. Repot in spring when roots fill the pot, usually every year when young.

✿ **Propagation:** Take 3in (7.5cm) stem-tip cuttings in spring. Place in 64–70°F (18–21°C).

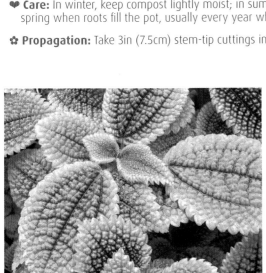

Moon Valley Plant
Pilea mollis

Also known as *Pilea* 'Moon Valley' and *Pilea involucrata* 'Moon Valley,' this small, bushy perennial has wrinkle-surfaced, oval- to pear-shaped, pointed leaves. They are yellowish-green, covered with minute white hairs, and contrasted by darker green veining. When young and unfurling, they are almost entirely maroon, with emerald-green edges.

↕ **Height:** 8–10in (20–25cm)

↔ **Spread:** 8–10in (20–25cm)

❋ **Winter:** 55–61°F (13–16°C). Direct light without full sun, or indirect light

✹ **Summer:** 61–75°F (16–24°C). Indirect light or light shade

❤ **Care:** In winter, keep compost lightly moist; in summer, water freely and feed every 2–3 weeks. Repot in spring when roots fill the pot, usually every year when young.

✿ **Propagation:** Take 3in (7.5cm) stem-tip cuttings in spring. Place in 64–70°F (18–21°C).

White-Edged Candle Plant, White-Edged Swedish Ivy
Plectranthus coleoides 'Marginatus'

Also known as *Plectranthus forsteri* 'Marginatus,' this evergreen perennial produces scalloped-edged, heart-shaped, hairy-surfaced, pale-green leaves with irregular white edges. Each leaf is 2–3in (5–7.5cm) wide.

↕ **Height:** 6–10in (15–25cm)

↔ **Spread:** 10–20in (25–50cm), spreading and trailing

❆ **Winter:** 45–50°F (7–10°C). Full sun, or direct light without full sun

☀ **Summer:** 55–70°F (13–21°C). Direct light without full sun

❤ **Care:** In winter, keep compost just moist; in summer, water freely and feed every 2 weeks. Repot in spring when roots fill the pot, usually every 2–3 years.

✿ **Propagation:** Take 3–4in (7.5–10cm) stem-tip cuttings during spring. Place them in 61–64°F (16–18°C).

Boat Lily, Men in a Boat, Moses in His Cradle, Moses in the Bulrushes, Moses on a Raft, Oyster Plant, Purple-Leaved Spiderwort, Two Men in a Boat, Three Men in a Boat
Rhoeo spathacea

Also known as *Tradescantia spathacea*, this evergreen perennial has stiff, lance-shaped, glossy dark-green leaves with rich purple undersides. 'Vittata' (sometimes sold as 'Vittatum' or 'Variegata') has leaves finely striped in cream.

↕ **Height:** 12–15in (30–38cm)

↔ **Spread:** 12in (30cm)

❆ **Winter:** 50–55°F (10–13°C). Indirect light

☀ **Summer:** 61–64°F (16–18°C). Indirect light or light shade

❤ **Care:** In winter, keep compost evenly moist; in summer, water freely and feed every 2–3 weeks. Repot in spring when roots fill the pot, usually every year when young.

✿ **Propagation:** Take 3–4in (7.5–10cm) long basal shoots in spring. Place them in 61–64°F (16–18°C).

Bowstring Hemp, Devil's Tongue, Good Luck Plant, Mother-in-Law's Tongue, Snake Plant
Sansevieria trifasciata

This evergreen succulent has upright, sword-like leaves. *Sansevieria trifasciata* has dark-green leaves with mottled gray transverse bands. *Sansevieria trifasciata* var. *laurentii* is more impressive, with bold, creamy yellow edges to the leaves. *Sansevieria trifasciata* 'Hahnii' (often sold as *Sansevieria hahnii*) is about 6in (15cm) high, with dark-green leaves that develop transverse gray and yellow bands. 'Golden Hahnii' has yellow edges to its leaves.

↕ **Height:** 15–18in (38–45cm)

↔ **Spread:** 6–8in (15–20cm)

❋ **Winter:** 45–50°F (7–10°C). Full sun

❋ **Summer:** 50–70°F (10–21°C). Full sun

❤ **Care:** In winter, keep compost barely moist; in summer, water thoroughly but allow to become slightly dry between applications, and feed every 2 weeks. Repot in spring, but only when the plant totally fills its pot with roots and stems, usually every 2–3 years.

❀ **Propagation:** All can be increased by dividing congested plants when being repotted, but those plants without yellow edges, such as *Sansevieria trifasciata,* can be also be increased by taking leaf cuttings during summer and placing them in 70°F (21°C).

Beefsteak Geranium, Creeping Sailor, Mother of Thousands, Pedlar's Basket, Rowing Sailor, Strawberry Begonia, Strawberry Geranium
Saxifraga stolonifera

Earlier known as *Saxifraga sarmentosa*, this tufted, trailing evergreen perennial has mid-green, round leaves with silvery veins. Their undersides are flushed red. Long, trailing, wiry stems bear plantlets at their tips, and white flowers appear during summer. 'Tricolor' has leaves variegated white, pink, and green, with red edges.

↕ **Height:** 8–10in (20–25cm)

↔ **Spread:** 10–15in (25–38cm) and trailing

❋ **Winter:** 41–50°F (5–10°C). Direct light without full sun

☀ **Summer:** 50–64°F (10–18°C). Indirect light

❤ **Care:** In winter, keep compost barely moist; in summer, water freely but ensure good drainage, and feed every 3–4 weeks. Repot in spring when roots fill the pot, usually every year for young and robustly growing plants.

✿ **Propagation:** Peg the plantlets into the compost in late spring and summer, and place in 50–64°F (10–18°C).

Australian Ivy Palm, Australian Umbrella Tree, Octopus Tree, Queensland Umbrella Tree, Rubber Tree, Star Leaf, Umbrella Plant, Umbrella Tree
Schefflera actinophylla

Earlier known as *Brassaia actinophylla*, this evergreen tree has leaves formed of leathery, glossy leaflets. Young plants have 3 leaflets to each leaf; more mature plants develop 5 or 7, each about 7in (18cm) long and 2in (5cm) wide.

↕ **Height:** 6–8ft (1.8–2.4m), sometimes more

↔ **Spread:** 2–3ft (60–90cm), sometimes more

❋ **Winter:** 50–55°F (10–13°C). Direct light without full sun

☀ **Summer:** 55–75°F (13–24°C). Indirect light

❤ **Care:** In winter, keep compost moderately moist; in summer, water more freely and feed every 3–4 weeks. Repot in spring when roots fill the pot, usually every 2–3 years. For large plants, top-dress the compost.

✿ **Propagation:** Sow seeds in late winter or early spring in seed trays. Place in 70–75°F (21–24°C).

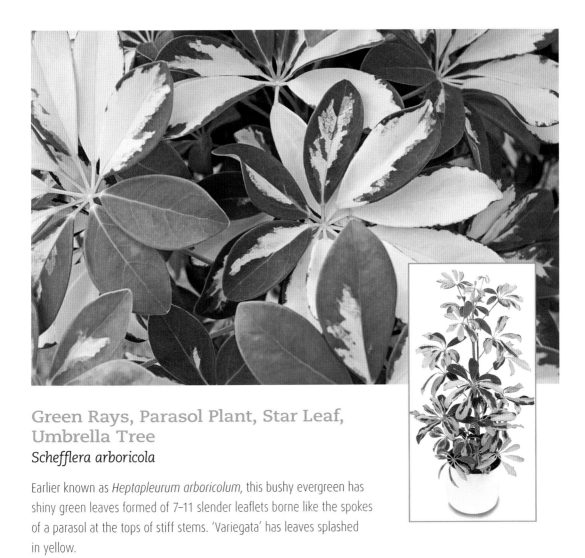

Green Rays, Parasol Plant, Star Leaf, Umbrella Tree
Schefflera arboricola

Earlier known as *Heptapleurum arboricolum*, this bushy evergreen has shiny green leaves formed of 7–11 slender leaflets borne like the spokes of a parasol at the tops of stiff stems. 'Variegata' has leaves splashed in yellow.

⇕ **Height:** 5–6ft (1.5–1.8m)

↔ **Spread:** 1 ½–2 ½ft (45–75cm)

❋ **Winter:** 55–59°F (13–15°C). Direct light without full sun

☀ **Summer:** 64–75°F (18–24°C). Indirect light

❤ **Care:** In winter, keep compost moderately moist; in summer, water freely but ensure good drainage, and feed every 3–4 weeks. Repot in spring when roots fill the pot, usually every 2–3 years. For large plants, top-dress the compost.

❀ **Propagation:** Sow seeds in late winter or early spring in seed trays. Place in 70–75°F (21–24°C).

Pick-a-Back Plant, Pig-a-Back Plant, Piggy-Back Plant, Thousand Mothers, Youth-on-Age
Tolmiea menziesii

Evergreen perennial with large, hairy, maple-like, mid-green leaves. Small plantlets grow where leafstalks join mature leaves. During summer it produces red-flushed, greenish-white flowers on long stems. There are several variegated forms, including 'Taff's Gold.'

↕ **Height:** 6–8in (15–20cm)

↔ **Spread:** 12–15in (30–38cm)

❄ **Winter:** 39–45°F (4–7°C). Direct light without full sun

☀ **Summer:** 50–64°F (10–18°C). Indirect light or light shade

❤ **Care:** In winter, keep compost evenly moist; in summer, water more freely and feed every 3 weeks. Repot in spring when roots fill the pot, usually every 1–2 years.

✿ **Propagation:** Divide congested plants in spring. Alternatively, in late spring or summer, sever mature leaves with plantlets attached to them and peg them on the compost surface. When plantlets have developed roots, transfer them to individual pots and place in 45–50°F (7–10°C). until established; later place in 50–64°F (10–18°C).

Inch Plant, Green Wandering Jew, Wandering Jew, Wandering Sailor, White-Flowered Spiderwort
Tradescantia fluminensis

Earlier known as *Tradescantia albiflora*, this evergreen perennial has trailing stems with oval green leaves that are 2–3in (5–7.5cm) long, stalkless, and appear to partially clasp the stem. Invariably, variegated forms are grown, including 'Albovittata' (leaves striped white), 'Aurea' (yellow with green stripes), and 'Tricolor Minima' (small leaves striped pink, white, and mauve).

↕ **Height:** 4–6in (10–15cm)

↔ **Spread:** Trailing

❄ **Winter:** 45–50°F (7–10°C). Direct light without full sun

☀ **Summer:** 50–64°F (10–18°C); avoid high temperatures. Indirect light

❤ **Care:** In winter, keep compost barely moist; in summer, water more freely and feed every 2–3 weeks. Repot in spring when roots fill the pot, usually every year when young.

✿ **Propagation:** Take 2–3in (5–7.5cm) stem-tip cuttings in summer. Place in 61°F (16°C).

Inch Plant, Silvery Inch Plant, Wandering Jew
Tradescantia zebrina

Also known as *Tradescantia pendula* and *Zebrina pendula*, this evergreen perennial has green leaves, 2–2½in (5–6.5cm) long, banded in glistening silver, with purple undersides. There are several forms, including 'Quadricolor' (leaves striped green, pink, red, and white) and 'Purpusii' (earlier known as *Zebrina purpusii* or *Zebrina pendula purpusii*), with leaves tinged purple.

‡ **Height:** 6–12in (15–30cm)

↔ **Spread:** Trailing

❉ **Winter:** 45–50°F (7–10°C). Direct light without full sun

✳ **Summer:** 50–70°F (10–21°C); avoid high temperatures. Indirect light

❤ **Care:** In winter, keep compost just moist; in summer, water more freely and feed every 2–3 weeks. Repot in spring when roots fill the pot, usually every 1–2 years.

❀ **Propagation:** Take 3in (7.5cm) stem-tip cuttings during summer. Place in 61–64°F (16–18°C).

Izote, Palm Lily, Spineless Yucca
Yucca elephantipes

Earlier known as *Yucca guatemalensis*, this tree-like evergreen develops stiff, green leaves up to 3ft (90cm) long, with rough edges. Old plants produce clusters of leaves at their tops, which has encouraged the common name, Palm Lily. Several other yuccas can be grown indoors, including *Yucca aloifolia* (Spanish Bayonet), which has stiff, sword-like leaves.

‡ **Height:** 3–6ft (90cm–1.8m)

↔ **Spread:** 1–2ft (30–60cm)

❉ **Winter:** 45–50°F (7–10°C); avoid high temperatures in winter. Full sun

✳ **Summer:** 50–64°F (10–18°C). Full sun, or direct light without full sun

❤ **Care:** In winter, keep compost barely moist; in summer, water more freely and feed every 3–4 weeks in summer. Repot in spring when roots fill the pot (though it naturally grows in small pots). Top-dress large plants that cannot be repotted.

❀ **Propagation:** Take 'log' cuttings (see pages 50–51) during summer. These are formed of 4in (10cm) cuttings taken from an old plant inserted in compost and placed in 61–64°F (16–18°C).

OTHER FOLIAGE HOUSEPLANTS

Aglaonema crispum (Painted Drop Tongue): this bushy, evergreen perennial has narrowly oval leaves, mostly silver, with greenish-gray parts.

Begonia metallica (Metallic-Leaf Begonia): fibrous roots, lopsided, triangular-shaped, metallic-green leaves, and distinctive purple veins.

Calathea lancifolia (Rattlesnake Plant): sometimes known as *Goepperitia lancifolia*, it displays long, narrow leaves with crinkly edges and yellowish background. Dark green bands radiate from the midrib.

Calathea zebrina (Zebra Plant): sometimes known as *Goepperitia zebrina*, with emerald-green leaves displaying horizontal dark-green stripes radiating from the midrib. Purple undersides.

Cordyline australis (Cabbage Tree, Fountain Grass, Giant Dracaena, Giant Fountain Grass, Grass Palm, Grass Plant, Palm Lily): earlier known as *Dracaena australis*, this evergreen perennial grows 25ft (7.5m) or more in the wild, but when young is an ideal houseplant. When young, it has a short stem with arching leaves. Some forms have colored or striped leaves.

Cyperus alternifolius (Umbrella Grass, Umbrella Plant): upright, stiff stems bear umbrella-like heads of slender, green, leaflike shoots.

Dracaena deremensis (Dragon Tree): narrow, ribbon-like, stiff, glossy-green leaves. Several variegated forms.

Dracaena godseffiana (Gold Dust Dracaena, Spotted Dracaena): also known as *Dracaena surculosa*, this woody shrub has a lax array of dark-green leaves spotted and splashed with cream.

Epipremnum aureum (Devil's Ivy, Pothos Vine): sometimes sold as *Scindapsus aureus*, its oval and pointed bright green leaves are splashed and streaked in yellow. Several attractive forms.

Episcia cupreata (Flame Violet): large, oval, soft, and copper-colored leaves with silvery veins; orange flowers in summer.

Ficus deltoidea (Mistletoe Fig, Mistletoe Rubber Plant, Mistletree): also known as *Ficus diversifolia*, this slow-growing evergreen shrub or small tree has leathery, dark-green, pear-shaped to oval leaves.

Fittonia verschaffeltii (Painted Net Leaf, Mosaic Plant): somewhat sprawling plant with dark-green leaves distinctively veined in carmine. Several attractive forms.

Grevillea robusta (Silky Oak): deep-green, fern-like leaves covered with silky hairs.

Gynura procumbens (Velvet Plant, Purple Passion Plant): twining and climbing plant with leaves covered with fine, purplish-hairs.

Iresine herbstii (Beef Plant, Beef Steak, Bloodleaf): evergreen perennial with a bushy nature and soft red stems that bear wine-red, heart-shaped leaves about 3in (7.5cm) long with paler red veining.

Pandanus sandieri perennial evergreen with stiff, arching, long and narrow, mid-green leaves that make it look stemless. Leaves are striped with thin, golden-yellow bands and have spiny edges.

Pandanus veitchii (Screw Pine, Veitch Screw Pine): evergreen perennial with narrow, spine-edged leaves that arch toward their tips. Initially forms a stemless rosette, but later has a stem. The dark-green leaves are striped and edged with white or creamy white flowers.

Peperomia argyreia (Rugby Football Plant, Silvered Peperomia, Watermelon Begonia): evergreen perennial with oval leaves that taper to a point. The smooth-surfaced leaves are a waxy, bluish-green with silver bands that radiate outward. Leafstalks are usually red.

Peperomia magnoliifolia (Desert Privet): evergreen perennial with a bushy nature and large, fleshy, green leaves. Best grown in one of its variegated forms, such as 'Variegata' (cream variegations) or 'Green and Gold' (cream edges to light-green leaves).

Pilea nummulariifolia (Creeping Charlie): evergreen perennial with a creeping, branching nature. Red, wiry stems branch and bear dark-green, rounded to heart-shaped leaves, with quilted surfaces. They are about ½in (12mm) wide.

FLOWERING HOUSEPLANTS

FLOWERING HOUSEPLANTS ARE MORE PERMANENT
FEATURES INDOORS THAN FLOWERING POTTED PLANTS,
WHICH HAVE AN EPHEMERAL NATURE (SEE PAGES 114-131).
WHEN THEY ARE NOT FLOWERING, THEY CAN BE PLACED IN
A CONSERVATORY OR HEATED GREENHOUSE, DEPENDING ON
THE TIME OF YEAR.

Chenille Plant, Foxtail, Philippine Medusa, Red Cattail, Red-Hot Cat's Tail
Acalypha hispida

Earlier known as *Acalypha sanderi,* this woody shrub
eventually needs a greenhouse border or large pot in a
conservatory, but is an ideal houseplant when young. It
produces bright scarlet flowers in long, pendulous tassels in
summer and into autumn. One of the forms is shown here.

↕ **Height:** 3–4ft (90cm–1.2m), up to 8ft (2.4m) or
more in a greenhouse border

↔ **Spread:** 1 ½–2 ½ft (45–75cm), up to 5ft (1.5m)
or more in a greenhouse border

❄ **Winter:** 59–64°F (15–18°C). Full sun

☀ **Summer:** 61–75°F (16–24°C). Bright light without
full sun

❤ **Care:** During winter, keep the compost slightly moist, but water freely in summer. Feed every 2 weeks
from late spring to late summer. Repot in late winter or early spring when roots fill the pot, usually every
2–3 years.

✿ **Propagation:** Take 4–5in (10–13cm) stem-tip cuttings in late spring or early summer and insert in equal
parts moist peat and sharp sand. Place in 61–75°F (16–24°C).

Basket Vine, Lipstick Plant, Lipstick Vine
Aeschynanthus radicans

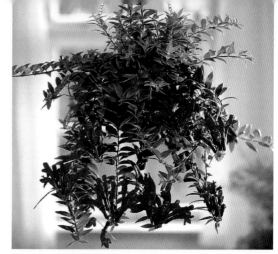

Lax, sprawling climber with small, oval, fleshy, dark-green leaves and tubular, hooded, bright red flowers with cream yellow throats during midsummer.

↕ Height: 1 ½–2ft (45–60cm)

✿ Winter: 55–59°F (13–15°C). Full sun

↔ Spread: 1 ½–2ft (45–60cm)—trailing

✸ Summer: 59–75°F (15–24°C). Full sun, or direct light without full sun

♥ Care: During winter, keep compost barely moist; in summer, water freely. From late spring to late summer feed every 4 weeks. Repot in spring when roots fill the pot, usually every 3 years.

✿ Propagation: Take 3in (7.5cm) stem-tip cuttings during midsummer and insert in equal parts moist peat and sharp sand. Place in 64–70°F (18–21°C).

Flaming Flower, Flamingo Flower, Flamingo Plant, Pigtail Flower, Pigtail Plant, Tail Flower
Anthurium scherzerianum

It has dark-green, heart-shaped leaves. Palette-shaped, brilliant scarlet spathes, 3–4in (7.5–10cm) long, appear throughout summer, with spiral, orange-red spadices (fleshy, stiff, usually brightly colored flower spikes).

↕ Height: 9–12in (23–30cm)

✿ Winter: 50–55°F (10–13°C). Indirect light

↔ Spread: 12–15in (30–38cm)

✸ Summer: 55–75°F (13–24°C). Light shade

♥ Care: In winter, keep compost barely moist but not dry; in summer, water freely but ensure good drainage. From late spring to late summer, feed every 2–3 weeks. Repot in spring when roots fill the pot, usually every 2–3 years.

✿ Propagation: Divide congested plants in spring. Place initially in 50–55°F (10–13°C).

Paper Flower
Bougainvillea x *buttiana* 'Mrs. Butt'

Deciduous climber with a vigorous nature. The flowers are insignificant; it is grown for its cascades of rose-crimson bracts that fade to magenta. There are many cultivars, with papery bracts lasting several months.

↕ **Height:** 5–8ft (1.5–2.4m) when grown in a large pot (more in border soil in a greenhouse)

↔ **Spread:** Climber

❄ **Winter:** 45–50°F (7–10°C). Full sun

☀ **Summer:** 50–70°F (10–21°C). Full sun, or direct light without full sun

❤ **Care:** In winter, keep compost slightly moist; in summer, water generously but ensure good drainage. From late spring to late summer, feed every 2–3 weeks. Repot in late winter or early spring when roots fill the pot, usually every year when young.

✿ **Propagation:** Take 3in (7.5cm) stem cuttings with heels (pieces of older wood attached to the cutting's base) during summer. Insert in equal parts moist peat and sharp sand. Place in 70°F (21°C).

Goldfish Plant
Columnea x *banksii*

Evergreen hybrid clothed in glossy, dark-green leaves. Orange-red flowers, about 3in (7.5cm) long, with orange markings in their throats, appear from early winter to mid-spring.

‡ **Height:** Long, trailing stems

↔ **Spread:** Trailer

❄ **Winter:** 55–61°F (13–16°C). Direct light without full sun

✺ **Summer:** 61–70°F (16–21°C). Indirect light

♥ **Care:** In winter, keep compost moist, especially when flowering; in summer, water freely but ensure good drainage. From late spring to late summer feed every 2–3 weeks. Repot in spring when roots fill the pot, usually every other year.

✿ **Propagation:** Take 3–4in (7.5–10cm)-long cuttings from nonflowering shoots during spring and early summer and insert in equal parts moist peat and sharp sand. Place in 64–70°F (18–21°C).

Cigar Flower, Cigar Plant, Firecracker Plant, Mexican Cigar Flower, Red-White-and-Blue Flower
Cuphea ignea

This short-lived evergreen has smooth-surfaced, lance-shaped, mid-green leaves. Masses of tubular, bright scarlet flowers, 1in (25mm) long, appear from late spring to early winter.

‡ **Height:** 12–15in (30–38cm), sometimes slightly more

↔ **Spread:** 12–15in (30–38cm), sometimes slightly more

❄ **Winter:** 45–50°F (7–10°C). Full sun, or direct light without full sun

✺ **Summer:** 50–64°F (10–18°C). Indirect light

♥ **Care:** In winter, keep compost barely moist; in summer, water freely and feed every 2–3 weeks. Repot established plants in spring when roots fill the pot, usually every 2–3 years.

✿ **Propagation:** Take 2–3in (5–7.5cm) stem-tip cuttings in late spring and insert in equal parts moist peat and sharp sand. Place in 61–64°F (16–18°C). Alternatively, sow seeds in late winter or spring, in 61°F (16°C).

Christ Plant, Christ Thorn, Crown of Thorns
Euphorbia millii

Earlier known as *Euphorbia splendens*, this tender, semi-succulent, semi-prostrate shrub has a woody nature and spiny stems. They are sparsely clad in pear-shaped, mid-green leaves, with flowers formed of two kidney-shaped, crimson bracts (modified leaves) throughout the year, but mostly in winter.

⬍ **Height:** 1–2ft (30–60cm)

↔ **Spread:** 1–2ft (30–60cm)

❄ **Winter:** 55°F (13°C). Full sun

☀ **Summer:** 55–61°F (13–16°C). Full sun, or direct light without full sun

❤ **Care:** In winter, keep compost barely moist; in summer, water freely and feed every 2 weeks. Repot in spring when roots fill the pot, usually every 2 years.

✿ **Propagation:** Take 3in (7.5cm) stem-tip cuttings in midsummer. Allow cut ends to dry before inserting them in equal parts moist peat and sharp sand. Place in 61–64°F (16–18°C).

Blacking Plant, China Rose, Chinese Hibiscus, Chinese Rose, Hawaiian Hibiscus, Rose of China, Shoe Black Plant
Hibiscus rosa-sinensis

Tender shrub with short-lived flowers, 5in (13cm) wide, from upper leaf-joints throughout summer. Normally, flowers are single and crimson, but semi-double and double forms are available in colors from creamy white to pale yellow. The dwarf form, 'Cooperi,' with crimson flowers and variegated leaves, is ideal for growing indoors.

⬍ **Height:** 1 ½–2ft (45–60cm) in a pot

↔ **Spread:** 15–18in (38–45cm) in a pot

❄ **Winter:** 45–50°F (7–10°C). Full sun

☀ **Summer:** 55–70°F (13–21°C). Direct light without full sun, or indirect light

❤ **Care:** In winter, keep compost barely moist; in summer, water freely but ensure good drainage, and feed every 2 weeks. Repot in spring when roots fill the pot, usually every year when young.

✿ **Propagation:** Take 3–4in (7.5–10cm) cuttings from nonflowering shoots in midsummer and insert in equal parts moist peat and sharp sand. Place in 64°F (18°C).

FRUITING AND BERRIED HOUSEPLANTS

Houseplants with berries and fruits remain attractive for a long time, especially if the room is cool. Most of these plants, such as *Ardisia crenata* and *Ficus deltoidea,* grow well in winter temperatures of 45–55°F (7–13°C), and slightly higher in summer, but citrus types benefit from a few degrees higher in both seasons. All prefer good light, but avoid extra-strong, direct sunlight in summer. Botanically, fruits and berries are different, but to most houseplant enthusiasts they are the same, ranging from bright red berries to orange-like fruits.

Coral Berry, Spice Berry
Ardisia crenata (also: *Ardisia crispa* and *Ardisia crenulata*)

This evergreen, shrub-like plant bears star-like, creamy white, fragrant flowers in early summer, followed by masses of long-lasting, glossy, scarlet berries.

Chili, Christmas Pepper, Green Pepper, Ornamental Pepper, Red Pepper
Capsicum annuum

Short-lived shrubby perennial usually grown as an annual; red, green, or yellow fruits during autumn and into winter.

Calamondin Orange, Panama Orange
X *Citrofortunella microcarpa* (also: *Citrofortunella mitis*)

This citrus plant bears fruits while still young and small. Highly scented white flowers appear throughout the year, followed by round fruits that slowly change from dark green to orange-yellow.

Chinese Dwarf Lemon, Dwarf Lemon, Meyer Lemon
Citrus x *meyeri* (also: *Citrus* x *limon* 'Meyer')

This is an ideal houseplant, with dark-green leaves and white, red-flushed, highly scented flowers in spring and early summer, followed by dark-green fruits that take several months to ripen.

Mistletoe Fig, Mistletoe Rubber Plant, Mistletree
Ficus deltoidea var. *diversifolia* (also: *Ficus diversifolia*)

This bushy, evergreen, slow-growing shrub or small tree has leathery, dark-green, pear-shaped to oval leaves. It gains its common names from the long-stalked, yellowish-gray, berry-like fruits borne from leaf-joints throughout the year.

Bead Plant
Nertera depressa (also: *Nertera granadensis*)

This clump-forming evergreen has creeping stems with oval to rounded, light-green leaves. Insignificant greenish-yellow flowers in early summer, followed by masses of glossy, bright orange berries in autumn and well into winter.

False Jerusalem Cherry, Winter Cherry
Solanum capsicastrum

Half-hardy, bushy, evergreen shrub usually grown as an annual indoors. Dark-green, lance-shaped leaves and insignificant, white, star-shaped flowers during early and midsummer, followed in winter by marble-like, slightly pointed, dark-green fruits that gradually change to yellow, then scarlet.

Honey Plant, Porcelain Flower, Wax Plant

Hoya carnosa

Vigorous evergreen climber with oval, fleshy, mid-green leaves. From early summer to early autumn it produces umbrella-like heads, 3in (7.5cm) wide, of fragrant, white to flesh-pink, star-like flowers. When young, plants can be trained around a hoop 10–12in (25–30cm) wide, but later need more substantial supports. There are several forms, including some with variegated leaves.

↕ **Height:** 8–15ft (2.4–4.5m) after several years   ↔ **Spread:** Climber

❄ **Winter:** 45–50°F (7–10°C). Direct light without full sun

☀ **Summer:** 61–70°F (16–21°C). Direct light without full sun, or indirect light

❤ **Care:** In winter, keep compost slightly moist; in summer, water freely if compost is well drained. Feed every 3 weeks from late spring to late summer. In late spring, repot plants with congested roots, usually every 2–3 years.

✿ **Propagation:** Take 3–4in (7.5–10cm) stem-tip cuttings during early and midsummer and insert in equal parts moist peat and sharp sand. Place in 61–64°F (16–18°C).

Jasmine, Pink Jasmine, Poet's Jassamine
Jasminum polyanthum

Slightly tender climber, with a twining nature and dark-green leaves formed of 5 or 7 leaflets. From early winter to late spring, it produces a wealth of strongly scented white, tubular flowers (pink when in bud) in lax clusters. When grown as a houseplant, it is usually bought twining around a circular, hooped framework, 10–12in (25–30cm) across. Later, and if transferred to a conservatory, it needs a large supporting framework.

↕ **Height:** 3–10ft (90cm–3m)

↔ **Spread:** Climber

❄ **Winter:** 50–55°F (10–13°C); survives temperatures down to 45°F (7°C), but is then reluctant to flower so early in the year. Full sun

☀ **Summer:** 55–64°F (13–18°C). Direct light without full sun, or indirect light

❤ **Care:** In early winter, keep compost moist and increase watering frequency as buds start to form; in summer, water freely. Feed every 2 weeks from when buds start to appear. Repot pot-bound plants after the flowers fade. Alternatively, plants in large pots can be top-dressed with fresh compost.

❀ **Propagation:** Take 3–4in (7.5–10cm) stem-tip cuttings in late spring and insert in equal parts moist peat and sharp sand. Place in 61–64°F (16–18°C).

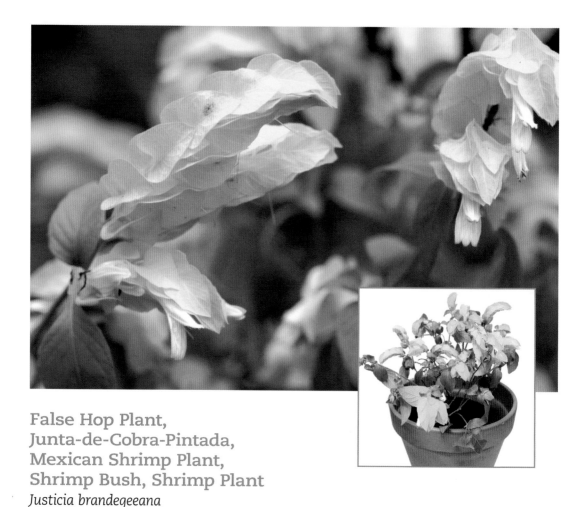

False Hop Plant,
Junta-de-Cobra-Pintada,
Mexican Shrimp Plant,
Shrimp Bush, Shrimp Plant
Justicia brandegeeana

Earlier known as *Beloperone guttata*, this distinctive shrub-like, evergreen perennial has soft green leaves and shrimp-like flowers formed of colorful bracts and inconspicuous white flowers from spring to midwinter.

↕ **Height:** 1 ½–2ft (45–60cm), sometimes more

↔ **Spread:** 1–1 ½ft (30–45cm), sometimes more

❄ **Winter:** 45–55°F (7–13°C). Direct light without full sun

☀ **Summer:** 55–75°F (13–24°C). Indirect light

❤ **Care:** In winter, keep compost barely moist, especially if the temperature falls; in summer, water compost freely. From late spring to late summer, feed every 2–3 weeks. Repot in early spring when roots fill the pot, usually every 2–3 years. Alternatively, top-dress plants in large pots with fresh compost.

✿ **Propagation:** Take 2–3in (5–7.5cm) cuttings in early spring and insert in equal parts moist peat and sharp sand. Place in 64–70°F (18–21°C).

Lollipop Plant
Pachystachys lutea

This tender, shrub-like plant has golden-yellow, poker-like heads throughout summer and into autumn. Flowers appear above the dark-green, narrowly oval to lance-shaped leaves.

⇕ **Height:** 15–18in (38–45cm)

↔ **Spread:** 12–15in (30–38cm)

❄ **Winter:** 55°F (13°C); can survive temperatures down to 50°F (10°C) if compost is kept slightly dry. Direct light without full sun

☀ **Summer:** 55–70°F (13–21°C). Indirect light

❤ **Care:** In winter, keep compost barely moist; in summer, water freely. Feed every 2 weeks from late spring to late summer. Repot when roots fill the pot, usually every year when young. Older plants can be top-dressed with fresh compost.

✿ **Propagation:** Take 4–5in (10–13cm) stem-tip cuttings in spring or early summer and insert in equal parts moist peat and sharp sand. Place in 70°F (21°C).

Peace Lily, Sail Plant, Spathe Flower
Spathiphyllum wallisii

This evergreen perennial has bright-green, lance-shaped leaves borne on long, stiff, upright stems. White, arum-like flowers appear from mid-spring to late summer. The hybrid *Spathiphyllum* 'Mauna Loa' produces larger, more brightly colored flowers.

⇕ **Height:** 9–12in (23–30cm)

↔ **Spread:** 12–15in (30–38cm)

❄ **Winter:** 50–55°F (10–13°C). Full sun

☀ **Summer:** 64–70°F (18–21°C). Direct light without full sun, or indirect light

❤ **Care:** In winter, keep compost evenly moist; in summer, water freely. Feed with weak fertilizer every 10–14 days from mid-spring to late summer. Feed every 4–5 weeks during the rest of the year. Repot when roots fill the pot, usually every year.

✿ **Propagation:** Divide congested plants in spring. Until established, place in 50–55°F (10–13°C).

INSECTIVOROUS HOUSEPLANTS

Insectivorous plants (*insectivores*) reveal how nature has adapted some plants to live in places where their roots cannot gain sufficient nutrients from the soil. Instead, adaptations allow them to trap and digest insects. Some, such as the Venus Fly Trap, use hinged jaws that snap shut when triggered by an insect, a few use sticky surfaces, and others have pitcher-like heads into which insects fall.

Insectivorous plants are not easy to grow indoors; they need to be watered with rainwater and kept in a humid atmosphere. They usually grow in marshy ground and need high humidity and indirect light. In winter, 50–55°F (10–13°C) suits them, with a few degrees higher in summer. They need light shade, especially in summer. Use clean rainwater to keep the compost slightly moist. If your home has a dry atmosphere, domed plastic covers create a humid environment for them.

FLY TRAPS

Venus Fly Trap
Dionaea muscipula

Forms a rosette of light-green leaves with hinged jaws. When a fly wanders into the open jaws, it touches trigger hairs that instantly close them. Digestive juices break down the insect's body and the plant absorbs the nutrients. Later, the hinged jaws open, ready to trap another fly.

STICKY-LEAVED PLANTS

Instead of jaws, these have sticky hairs and are known as sundews. These are a few of many different species.

Giant Fork-Leaved Sundew
Drosera binata

Leaves divide at their tops into 2 or 4 segments; sticky hairs trap and digest insects.

Sundew
Drosera capensis

Leaf rosettes covered with red hairs trap and digest insects; purple flowers on stems up to 15in (38cm) high.

Round-Leaved Sundew
Drosera rotundifolia

Small plant with long-stemmed, round leaves covered with fine, red hairs; glands on the leaves exude clear drops of fluid resembling small dew drops.

PITCHER PLANTS (HOODED AND LIDDED)

Californian Pitcher Plant, Cobra Lily, Cobra Orchid, Hooded Pitcher Plant
Darlingtonia californica

Hooded pitcher plant resembling a cobra's head; heavily veined, yellowish or pale green, up to 2ft (60cm) high.

Pitcher Plant
Nepenthes x coccinea

Lidded type, with brightly colored pitchers. Best positioned in an indoor hanging basket, or a pot on a shelf, so the pitchers hang freely. Insects fall in and are digested.

Huntsman's Horn, Trumpet Leaf, Umbrella Trumpets, Watches, Yellow Pitcher Plant
Sarracenia flava

Long, yellow-green pitchers with purple or crimson veining in their throats. Each has an erect lid. Insects fall into the pitcher and are digested.

Huntsman's Cup, Indian Cup, Pitcher Plant, Side-Saddle Flower
Sarracenia purpurea

Purple and green pitchers (resembling raw meat) attract flies, which fall inside and are digested.

Floradora, Madagascar Jasmine, Wax Flower
Stephanotis floribunda

This tender, evergreen twining, climbing shrub has dark-green, leathery, oval leaves about 3in (7.5cm) long. In summer and into autumn, it produces heads of up to 8 exquisitely scented, waxy-white flowers, 1 ½in (36mm) long. When young, it can be grown over a 10–12in (25–30cm) hoop-like frame; later more substantial support is needed.

↕ **Height:** 10ft (3m) when in a conservatory; initially, and when in a pot 6–8in (15–20cm) wide, it is much smaller—often no more than 18in (45cm) high

↔ **Spread:** Climber

❄ **Winter:** 50–55°F (10–13°C). Direct light without full sun

☀ **Summer:** 64–70°F (18–21°C). Direct light without full sun, or indirect light

❤ **Care:** In winter, keep compost slightly moist; in summer, water freely but ensure it is well drained. Feed every 2–3 weeks from late spring to late summer. Repot in spring when roots fill the pot, initially every year, but later every 2–3 years.

❀ **Propagation:** Take 4in (10cm) cuttings from side-shoots in late spring or early summer and insert in equal parts moist peat and sharp sand. Place in 70°F (21°C).

Cape Primrose
Streptocarpus x *hybridus*

These evergreen, tufted hybrids are derived from a wide range of streptocarpus species and are well known for their long, spoon-shaped, mid-green and corrugated leaves. They bear foxglove-like flowers, 1 ½–2 ½in (36–60mm) long, in small clusters from early summer to autumn. The wide color range includes white, red, and purple. 'Constant Nymph' has satiny, bluish-purple flowers.

↕ **Height:** 8–12in (20–30cm)

↔ **Spread:** 9–15in (23–38cm)

❄ **Winter:** 50–55°F (10–13°C). Direct light without full sun

☀ **Summer:** 55–59°F (13–15°C). Direct light without full sun

❤ **Care:** In winter, keep compost just moist; in summer, water freely but ensure good drainage. Feed every 2–3 weeks from late spring to late summer. Repot in spring when roots fill the pot, usually every 2–3 years.

❀ **Propagation:** Divide congested plants in spring, initially placing them in 50–55°F (10–13°C). Alternatively, take leaf cuttings in midsummer and place in 55–61°F (13–16°C). Avoid high temperatures.

OTHER FLOWERING HOUSEPLANTS

Allamanda cathartica (Golden Trumpet): climber with golden-yellow flowers during summer amid long, leathery, glossy green leaves. Several superb cultivars, including 'Hendersonii' (large, orange-yellow flowers) and 'Grandiflora' (pale-yellow flowers).

Brunfelsia pauciflora (Yesterday, Today, and Tomorrow): earlier known as *Brunfelsia calycina*, this evergreen shrub has mid-green, shiny leaves and fragrant, violet-purple flowers with white throats from spring to autumn.

Crossandra infundibuliformis (Firecracker Flower): earlier known as *Crossandra undulifolia*, this evergreen shrub has wavy-edged, dark-green leaves and clusters of orange-red flowers from spring to autumn.

Gardenia jasminoides (Cape Jasmine): earlier known as *Gardenia augusta*, this tender evergreen shrub has highly fragrant, waxy white flowers, 3in (7.5cm) wide, from early to late summer.

Ixora coccinea (Flame of the Woods, Burning Love, Jungle Geranium): evergreen shrub with large heads, up to 4in (10cm) across, packed with tubular flowers in red, pink, salmon, yellow, or white throughout summer.

Plumbago auriculata
(Cape Leadwort)

Justicia carnea (King's Crown, Brazilian Plume, Paradise Plant): earlier known as *Jacobinia carnea*, this evergreen shrub has plume-like heads of pink, tubular flowers in late summer and early autumn.

Mandevilla splendens: earlier known as *Diplandenia splendens*, this twining, evergreen shrub bears 6–8in (15–20cm) clusters of rose-pink, trumpet-shaped flowers from early to late summer, sometimes into early autumn.

Plumbago auriculata (Cape Leadwort): earlier known as *Plumbago capensis*, this evergreen climber has star-shaped, tubular, sky-blue flowers during summer and into autumn.

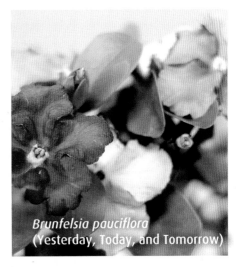

Brunfelsia pauciflora
(Yesterday, Today, and Tomorrow)

FLOWERING
POTTED PLANTS

FLOWERING POTTED PLANTS ARE THE MOST WIDELY GROWN OF ALL INDOOR PLANTS. EACH YEAR VAST NUMBERS ARE BOUGHT WHEN THEIR COLORFUL DISPLAY BEGINS, THEN DISCARDED WHEN IT IS OVER. THEY MAKE SUPERB PRESENTS, AND MANY ENTHUSIASTS TRY TO GROW THEM FOR A SECOND YEAR, BUT THE DISPLAY IS OFTEN DISAPPOINTING.

Cupid's Bower, Hot Water Plant, Monkey-Faced Pansy, Mother's Tears, Widow's Tears
Achimenes hybrids

From early to late summer, these hybrids bear masses of trumpet-like flowers. Colors include white, pink, red, purple, and blue. Each flower is short-lived, but soon replaced by others.

↕ **Height:** 12–15in (30–38cm)

↔ **Spread:** 10–12in (25–30cm)

❄ **Winter:** Not applicable

☀ **Summer:** 55–59°F (13–15°C). Direct light without full sun, or indirect light

❤ **Care:** In summer, water freely but ensure compost is well drained, and feed every 2–3 weeks.

✿ **Propagation:** Plants can be raised from tuber-like rhizomes, but fresh plants are usually bought each year.

Perennial Spiraea
Astilbe x arendsii

Astilbes are hardy herbaceous perennials, sometimes encouraged in garden centers to flower indoors for about a month during late winter and early spring, which is earlier than their normal summer-flowering period outdoors. They have deep-green, fern-like leaves and flowers borne in plume-like heads in colors such as clear pink, dark red, salmon-red, and white.

⭥ **Height:** 1 ½–2ft (45–60cm)

↔ **Spread:** 15–18in (38–45cm)

❆ **Winter:** 50–55°F (10–13°C). Direct light without full sun

✳ **Summer:** Not applicable

💙 **Care:** Keep compost moist, especially when the plant is flowering. No feeding is needed. After flowering, either discard or transfer to a garden border.

✿ **Propagation:** Buy new plants each year.

Azalea, Indian Azalea
Azalea indica

Properly known as *Rhododendron simsii*, this small, bushy, evergreen shrub is encouraged in garden centers to flower from mid- to late winter. The small, narrowly oval to pear-shaped, dark-green leaves create an attractive background for the funnel-shaped flowers. Colors include crimson, salmon, pink, and white, in single- and double-flowered forms. There are also bicolored forms.

⭥ **Height:** 1–1 ½ft (30–45cm) when in a pot

↔ **Spread:** 15–18in (38–45cm) when in a pot

❆ **Winter:** 50–59°F (10–15°C); avoid high temperatures. Direct light without full sun, or indirect light

✳ **Summer:** Not applicable

💙 **Care:** Keep compost moist when the plant is flowering. No feeding is needed. After flowering, it can be planted in a garden.

✿ **Propagation:** Buy fresh plants each year.

Hybrid Tuberous Begonia, Tuberous Begonia, Tuberous-Rooted Begonia
Begonia x *tuberhybrida*

Also known as *Begonia* Tuberhybrida Hybrids, these floriferous, tuberous-rooted plants have mid-green leaves and large, rose-like flowers from early summer to early autumn. Apart from being grown as houseplants, they can be planted in gardens for summer flowering. Individual flowers are 3–6in (7.5–15cm) across, in colors including scarlet, rose-pink, golden-yellow, crimson, and orange.

↕ **Height:** 12–20in (30–50cm)

↔ **Spread:** 12–15in (30–38cm)

❆ **Winter:** Not applicable, unless increasing your own plants (see below)

☀ **Summer:** 55–64°F (13–18°C); avoid high temperatures. Direct light without full sun, or indirect light

❤ **Care:** When in flower, keep compost moist, but not waterlogged, and feed every 2–3 weeks.

✿ **Propagation:** Buy fresh plants each year, or put tubers in boxes of moist peat in 64°F (18°C) in early or mid-spring. When shoots develop, transfer the tubers to individual pots and lower the temperature slightly to 55°F (13°C). Later, place in 55–64°F (13–18°C).

Pocketbook Flower, Pouch Flower, Slipper Flower, Slipper Plant
Calceolaria x *herbeohybrida*

These tender hybrids exhibit bushy growth and masses of pouch-like flowers from late spring to midsummer when indoors. Colors include shades of yellow, orange, and red, either spotted or blotched in crimson.

↕ **Height:** 8–18in (20–45cm)

↔ **Spread:** 8–15in (20–38cm)

❆ **Winter:** Not applicable

☀ **Summer:** 50–59°F (10–15°C); avoid high temperatures. Direct light without full sun

❤ **Care:** When flowering, keep compost moist and feed every 2 weeks. Discard plants after flowering and replace the following year.

✿ **Propagation:** Plants are biennial, raised from seed sown in midsummer and overwintered as young plants.

Feathered Amaranth, Plume Flower, Plumed Cock's Flower, Prince of Wales' Feather
Celosia argentea 'Plumosa'

Brightly colored, pyramidal, and feathery spires of flowers, 3–6in (7.5–15cm) high, appear from mid- to late summer. Colors include pink, yellow, crimson, and amber. *Celosia argentea* 'Venezuela' is another attractive form (pictured below).

‡ **Height:** 12–15in (30–38cm)

❄ **Winter:** Not applicable

↔ **Spread:** 8–10in (20–25cm)

✳ **Summer:** 55–59°F (13–15°C); avoid high temperatures. Direct light without full sun

❤ **Care:** When flowering, keep compost moist and feed every 2–3 weeks. Discard plants after flowering.

❀ **Propagation:** Sow seeds in 64°F (18°C) in greenhouses in late winter.

Chrysanthemum: All-Year-Round Types

Popular flowering plants, available throughout the year either in pots or as cut flowers. Traditionally, they flower in late summer and through to midwinter, but young plants can be encouraged to flower at any time of the year by providing them with strict regimes of dark and light, and suitable temperatures. Nurseries also use chemicals to produce smaller plants. There are single- and double-flowered types in colors such as yellow, orange, red, pink, and white.

‡ **Height:** 8–15in (20–38cm) when in pots

❄ **Winter:** 50–61°F (10–16°C); avoid high temperatures. Direct light without full sun

↔ **Spread:** 10–20in (25–50cm) when in pots

✳ **Summer:** 50–61°F (10–16°C); avoid high temperatures. Indirect light

❤ **Care:** When flowering, keep compost moist. Neither feeding nor repotting is necessary. These plants remain in flower for several months but are best discarded after blooming.

❀ **Propagation:** Buy fresh plants throughout the year.

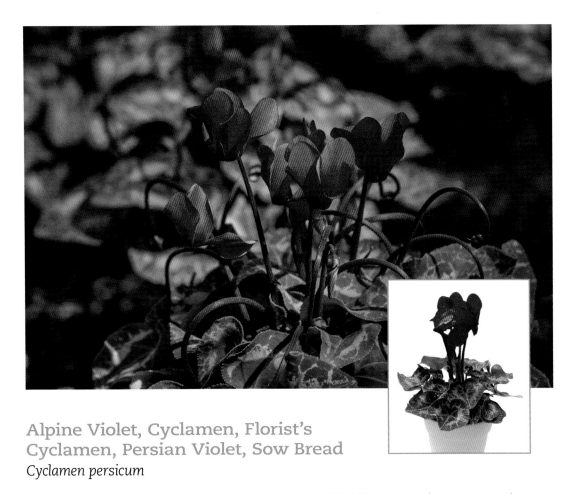

Alpine Violet, Cyclamen, Florist's Cyclamen, Persian Violet, Sow Bread
Cyclamen persicum

Popular houseplant sold from early autumn to spring. Shuttlecock-like flowers, some fragrant, appear above round, marble-colored leaves. Colors include pink, white, or red, and pastel shades.

↕ **Height:** There are several strains, including standard (about 12in [30cm] high), intermediate (about 9in [23cm] high), and miniature (about 6in [15cm] high)

↔ **Spread:** See above; most plants are about the same width as they are high

❄ **Winter:** 55–59°F (13–15°C) from when buds show color. Direct light without full sun, or indirect light

☀ **Summer:** 55–59°F (13–15°C). Indirect light

❤ **Care:** When flowering or buds are showing color, keep compost moist and feed every 2–3 weeks. Most plants are discarded after the flowers fade, but if you decide to keep the plant, reduce the amount of water, gradually drying off the corm (still in the compost and pot), and place in a cool, airy place. In late summer, repot into a clean pot and fresh compost. Water the compost and place in a cool, bright greenhouse. When shoots and leaves start to develop, slowly increase the temperature and amount of water.

✿ **Propagation:** Plants can be raised from seeds, but this is best left to experts as it takes 12–15 months to produce large plants.

Cape Heath, Winter-Flowering Erica
Erica gracilis

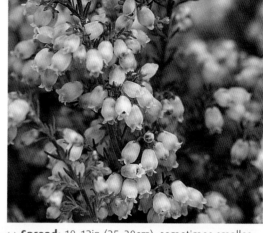

Evergreen, ericaceous plant with spires of pale-green leaves and tubular to globe-shaped, rosy-purple flowers in autumn and winter. There is also a white-flowered form.

↕ **Height:** 1–1 ½ft (30–45cm), sometimes smaller

↔ **Spread:** 10–12in (25–30cm), sometimes smaller

❄ **Winter:** 41–45°F (5–7°C); avoid high temperatures. Full sun, or direct light without full sun

☀ **Summer:** Not applicable

❤ **Care:** Use lime-free water and keep compost moist but not waterlogged. No feeding is needed.

❀ **Propagation:** Discard plants after flowering (though they can be planted outdoors in warm, temperate climates).

French Heather, White Winter Heather, Winter-Flowering Erica
Erica x hiemalis

Sometimes listed as *Erica hyemalis*, this ericaceous shrub has mid-green, thread-like leaves. Tubular flowers, white with a pink flush, are borne in terminal clusters from late autumn to late winter.

↕ **Height:** 15–18in (38–45cm), sometimes slightly more

↔ **Spread:** 10–12in (25–30cm), sometimes slightly more

❄ **Winter:** 41–45°F (5–7°C); avoid high temperatures. Full sun, or direct light without full sun

☀ **Summer:** Not applicable

❤ **Care:** Use lime-free water and keep compost moist but not waterlogged. No feeding is needed.

❀ **Propagation:** Discard plants after flowering (though they can be planted outdoors in warm, temperate climates).

Christmas Star, Lobster Plant, Mexican Flameleaf, Painted Leaf, Poinsettia
Euphorbia pulcherrima

This well-known late-autumn to late-winter flowering houseplant has colorful, leaflike bracts up to 6in (15cm) long, usually bright crimson, though scarlet, white, pink, and cream forms are also available.

↕ **Height:** 12–18in (30–45cm)

↔ **Spread:** 12–18in (30–45cm)

❄ **Winter:** 55–61°F (15–16°C); avoid high temperatures. Indirect light

✹ **Summer:** Not applicable

❤ **Care:** Keep compost evenly moist, but not waterlogged. No feeding is needed. Poinsettias can be kept from one year to another, but because garden centers use chemicals to produce compact and dwarf plants, they may be larger the following year. In practical terms, plants are best discarded.

✿ **Propagation:** Buy a new plant the following year.

Arabian Violet, German Violet, Mexican Violet, Persian Violet
Exacum affine

Bushy plant with small, glossy, oval leaves and fragrant, violet flowers with yellow stamens from mid- to late summer.

↕ **Height:** 6–10in (15–25cm)

↔ **Spread:** 6–10in (15–25cm)

❄ **Winter:** Not applicable

✹ **Summer:** 55–61°F (13–16°C); avoid high temperatures. Direct light without full sun

❤ **Care:** Keep compost moist, but not continually saturated. Feed every 10 days with weak liquid fertilizer from when buds show color to when the flowers fade.

✿ **Propagation:** Discard plants after their flowers fade.

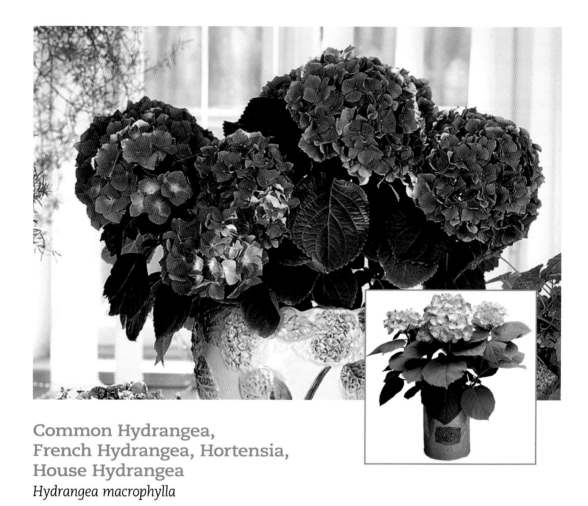

Common Hydrangea, French Hydrangea, Hortensia, House Hydrangea
Hydrangea macrophylla

There are two types of *Hydrangea macrophylla*: the Mop-head type (sometimes known as Hortensia, with large, round flower heads 6–8in [15–20cm] wide) and the Lacecaps (flat, more open heads, 4–6in [10–15cm] wide). The Mop-head type is grown as a houseplant, in colors including white, blue, pink, and red. They are ideal for introducing color to cool rooms during late spring and early summer. Most are bought when just beginning to show color. Outdoors, they flower from midsummer to autumn.

↕ **Height:** 1–1 ½ft (30–45cm) in pots indoors

↔ **Spread:** 1–1 ½ft (30–45cm) in pots indoors

❄ **Winter:** Not applicable if plants are bought in spring

☀ **Summer:** 45–50°F (7–10°C). Indirect light

❤ **Care:** When in flower, keep compost moist but not waterlogged. Feed every 10 days from when buds form until flowers fade. No repotting is necessary. They are usually planted in a garden when their flowers fade.

✿ **Propagation:** Buy plants in spring.

Busy Lizzie, Patience Plant, Patience Plant, Patient Lucy, Sultana, Zanzibar Balsam
Impatiens walleriana

Earlier known as *Impatiens sultani*, this is one of the most popular houseplants. It is sometimes classified as a flowering houseplant because it lives from one year to another, but usually becomes leggy and is replaced every year. It has flat-faced, 5-petaled flowers in colors such as pink, red, purple, orange, and white. There are many hybrids in mixed colors, some with variegated leaves.

↕ **Height:** 1–2ft (30–60cm)

❄ **Winter:** 55°F (13°C); it can withstand temperatures down to 45°F (7°C) if the compost is kept slightly drier. Full sun, or direct light without full sun

↔ **Spread:** 15–18in (30–45cm)

☀ **Summer:** 61–64°F (16–18°C). Direct light without full sun

❤ **Care:** Keep compost moist, but not waterlogged. From late spring to late summer, feed every week with weak liquid fertilizer. No repotting is needed if plants are discarded each year.

❀ **Propagation:** Take 3–4in (7.5–10cm) stem-tip cuttings from late spring to late summer and insert in equal parts moist peat and sharp sand. Place in 61°F (16°C). Alternatively, buy fresh plants each year.

Flaming Katy
Kalanchoe blossfeldiana

Thick, succulent, dark-green leaves with scalloped edges. By manipulating periods of light and dark, combined with suitable temperatures, nurseries can produce flowering plants throughout the year. Each remains in flower for 6 weeks or more, then is discarded. Colors include red, white, yellow, orange, and lilac.

↕ **Height:** 8–10in (20–25cm)

❄ **Winter:** 50–55°F (10–13°C). Full sun

↔ **Spread:** 8–10in (20–25cm)

☀ **Summer:** 55–64°F (13–18°C). Direct light without full sun, or indirect light

❤ **Care:** Water compost thoroughly, but allow to dry out slightly between waterings. From when buds show color, feed every 2–3 weeks.

❀ **Propagation:** Buy plants throughout the year and discard after flowering.

Baby Primula, Fairy Primrose, Fairy Primula
Primula malacoides

Winter- and spring-flowering perennial, but usually grown as a greenhouse annual, it has pale-green, oval leaves. Whorls of star-like flowers appear in several colors—pink, carmine-red, white, lavender, and white, with yellow eyes.

↕ **Height:** 12–15in (30–38cm)

↔ **Spread:** 12–15in (30–38cm)

❄ **Winter:** 45–50°F (7–10°C). Direct light without full sun, or indirect light

☀ **Summer:** Not applicable

❤ **Care:** When flowering, keep compost moist but not waterlogged. From when flower buds appear, feed every 10–14 days with weak liquid fertilizer. Discard plants when they cease flowering.

✿ **Propagation:** Buy fresh plants each year, or sow seeds during summer and place in a cold frame or greenhouse at 45°F (7°C). Barely cover seeds with compost.

German Primrose, Poison Primrose
Primula obconica

Although this is a greenhouse perennial, fresh plants are invariably raised as annuals, flowering from early winter to late spring. Clusters of flowers, 1in (25mm) wide, appear in pink, red, lilac, or blue-purple. The light-green, oval to heart-shaped leaves form an attractive backdrop for the flowers, but can create painful rashes, especially on wrists and arms, especially when damp.

⇕ **Height:** 9–15in (23–38cm)

↔ **Spread:** 9–15in (23–38cm)

❄ **Winter:** 45–50°F (7–10°C). Direct light without full sun, or indirect light

❋ **Summer:** Not applicable

❤ **Care:** When flowering, keep compost moist but not waterlogged. From when flower buds appear, feed every 10–14 days with weak liquid fertilizer. Discard plants when flowers fade.

❀ **Propagation:** Buy fresh plants each year, or sow seeds during late spring and early summer and place in 59–68°F (15–20°C).

Chinese Primrose
Primula sinensis

Tender greenhouse perennial that is grown as a greenhouse annual in temperate areas. It has bright-green, lobed, tooth-edged hairy leaves. Flowers, 1–1 ½in (25–36mm) wide, are borne in clusters from midwinter to early spring. Some have frilly edges. Colors include white, pink, red, orange, and purple. Like *Primula obconica*, the leaves can cause rashes on arms and wrists, especially when damp.

⇕ **Height:** 10in (25cm)

↔ **Spread:** 8–10in (20–25cm)

❄ **Winter:** 50°F (10°C); avoid high temperatures. Direct light without full sun, or indirect light

❋ **Summer:** Not applicable, unless raising your own plants from seeds (see below)

❤ **Care:** When flowering, keep compost moist but not waterlogged. From when flower buds appear, feed every 10–14 days with weak liquid fertilizer. No repotting is necessary.

❀ **Propagation:** Sow seeds in seed trays from late spring to midsummer. Place in a cold frame at 45°F (7°C). Barely cover seeds with compost.

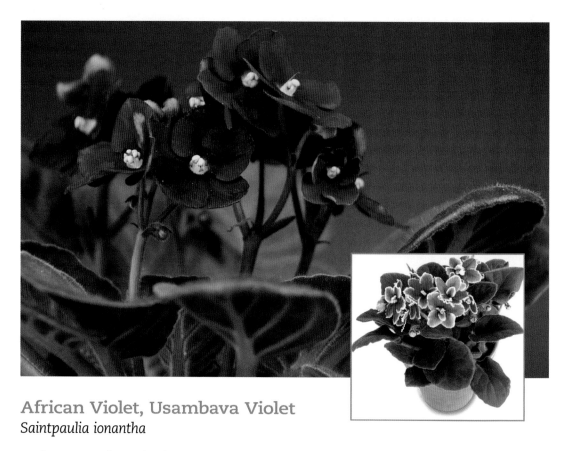

African Violet, Usambava Violet
Saintpaulia ionantha

Small, evergreen plant with velvet-textured, dark- to mid-green, heart-shaped leaves and small purple, violet-like flowers with bright golden-yellow eyes, mainly from early summer to early autumn. There are many strains and nowadays you can have African Violets in flower at any time of year. The range of flower types includes single, semi-double, double, frilled, star, bicolor, and multicolor. Some have all-green leaves, others are variegated, spoon-edged, or serrated. There are also trailing types.

‡ **Height:** About ⅔ of the spread (see below)

↔ **Spread:** Micro-miniatures: less than 3in (7.5cm); miniatures: 3–6in (7.5–15cm); semi-miniatures: 6–8in (15–20cm); standard varieties: 15in (38cm); large varieties: more than 15in (38cm)

❅ **Winter:** 59–64°F (15–18°C). Full sun, or direct light without full sun

✳ **Summer:** 59–64°F (15–18°C). Direct light without full sun

❤ **Care:** Keep compost moist in summer and winter, but not continually saturated. From late spring to late summer, feed every 2 weeks with weak liquid fertilizer. No repotting is necessary.

✿ **Propagation:** Take leaf-stem cuttings during summer and insert leaf-stems in equal parts moist peat and sharp sand. Place in 64–70°F (18–24°C).

Butterfly Flower, Poor Man's Orchid
Schizanthus pinnatus

This bushy annual is grown as a half-hardy annual in temperate climates. During spring and early summer, plants produce masses of orchid-like flowers amid pale-green, almost fern-like leaves. Flower colors include yellow, purple, and rose, with attractive markings and spots. These plants can also be grown outdoors in warm, temperate climates, when they flower from midsummer to early autumn.

↕ **Height:** 1–2 ½ft (30–75cm)—range of cultivars

↔ **Spread:** 10–15in (25–38cm)—range of cultivars

❄ **Winter:** 45–50°F (7–10°C). Full sun

✳ **Summer:** 45–55°F (7–13°C). Direct light without full sun

❤ **Care:** Keep compost moist, especially when the plant is flowering. From when flower buds show color to when they fade, feed every 10 days with weak liquid fertilizer. Discard after flowering.

✿ **Propagation:** Sow seeds in late summer in seed trays. Place in 59–68°F (15–20°C).

Cineraria, Florist's Cineraria
Senecio cruentus

Botanically known as *Pericallis* x *hybrida*, and earlier as *Cineraria cruenta* and *Cineraria* x *hybrida*, it produces masses of large, daisy-like flowers in flat or domed heads from late winter to midsummer. White, blue, purple, pink, and red flowers appear above mid-green, somewhat heart-shaped leaves up to 8in (20cm) across. Flower shapes vary. Grandiflora types have individual flowers 2–3in (5–7.5cm) wide on plants 1 ½–2ft (45–60cm) high; Multiflora Nana types have flowers 1–2in (25–50mm) wide on plants 9–15in (23–38cm) high; double-flowered forms have flowers about 2in (5cm) wide on plants 1–2ft (30–60cm) high. Stellata types have star-like flowers 1–1 ½in (25–36mm) wide on plants about 2ft (60cm) high.

⇕ **Height:** See above

↔ **Spread:** See above; most plants are about the same width as they are high

❄ **Winter:** 50–59°F (10–15°C); avoid high temperatures. Direct light without full sun

☀ **Summer:** 50–59°F (10–15°C); avoid high temperatures. Indirect light

❤ **Care:** Keep compost moist, especially when the plant is flowering. Feeding is not usually necessary, but you can produce larger plants by giving weak liquid fertilizer every 2 weeks from when the flowers show color. Discard plants when flowers fade.

✿ **Propagation:** Buy fresh plants each year.

Cardinal Flower
Sinningia cardinalis

Earlier known as *Rechsteineria cardinalis* and *Gesneria cardinalis*, this tuberous-rooted plant has spectacular, hooded, bright scarlet flowers with paler throats. They are 2in (5cm) long, borne in terminal clusters from early to late summer. The velvet-surfaced leaves are broadly oval and 4in (10cm) long.

↕ **Height:** 9–18in (23–45cm)

↔ **Spread:** 10–12in (25–30cm)

❋ **Winter:** Not applicable

❋ **Summer:** 61–64°F (16–18°C). Direct light without full sun, or indirect light

♥ **Care:** Keep compost moist but not waterlogged while the plant is flowering. If you decide not to discard the plant when flowers fade and leaves turn yellow, gradually cease watering, remove dead leaves and flowers and store tubers in 55°F (13°C) in a dry, airy place. Restart into growth in spring in 21°C (70°F), slowly increasing the amount of water. No feeding is necessary.

✿ **Propagation:** Buy fresh plants each year.

Brazilian Gloxinia, Florist's Gloxinia, Gloxinia, Violet Slipper Gloxinia
Sinningia speciosa

Earlier known as *Gloxinia speciosa*, this tuberous-rooted plant has fleshy, velvety, almost stemless, large, oblong, dark-green leaves up to 8in (20cm) long. Bell-shaped flowers, 2–4in (5–10cm) long and 3in (7.5cm) across, appear from late spring to late summer. Colors include violet and purple. There are several named cultivars in white, red, pink, and purple, some with colored or crimped edges. Most Gloxinias are bought when buds are just showing color, and flowers continue for 8 or more weeks.

↕ **Height:** 9–14in (23–35cm)

↔ **Spread:** 10–12in (25–30cm)

❋ **Winter:** Not applicable if plants are bought when in flower

❋ **Summer:** 64°F (18°C). Indirect light

♥ **Care:** From late spring to late summer, keep compost moist, but not waterlogged. Feed every 2 weeks with weak liquid fertilizer from when the buds show color.

✿ **Propagation:** In late winter, place dormant tubers in boxes of moist peat in 70°F (21°C). When shoots are about 1 ½in (36mm) high, pot each tuber into an individual pot. However, it is simpler to buy fresh plants each year.

Temple Bells
Smithiantha hybrids

Tender, rhizomatous hybrids mainly derived from *Smithiantha cinnabarina* and *Smithiantha zebrina.* They have dark-green, heart-shaped leaves and many pendulous, long and bell-shaped, foxglove-like flowers in shades of white, yellow-red, orange, and pink (many with purple markings). They are borne on large, pyramidal heads from early to late summer.

↕ Height: 1 ½–2ft (45–60cm)

❋ Winter: 64–70°F (18–21°C). Full sun

↔ Spread: 1–1 ½ft (30–45cm)

❅ Summer: 64–70°F (18–21°C). Direct light without full sun, or indirect light

❤ Care: From early to late summer, keep compost moist, but not waterlogged. No feeding is necessary.

✿ Propagation: Divide congested rhizomes at potting time, from late winter to late spring and place in 64–70°F (18–21°C). Alternatively, take leaf cuttings in late spring or early summer and place in 70°F (21°C).

Black-Eyed Susan Vine
Thunbergia alata

Well-known climbing garden plant in temperate climates but also superb indoors for creating a colorful screen. During summer, it has white, yellow, or orange flowers, each with a black eye, amid oval, mid-green leaves.

↕ Height: 3–4ft (90cm–1.2m)

❋ Winter: Not applicable

↔ Spread: 1 ½–2ft (45–60cm), sometimes more

❅ Summer: 50–61°F (10–16°C); avoid high temperatures. Direct light without full sun

❤ Care: In summer, keep compost moist but not waterlogged. From when the buds show color, feed with weak liquid fertilizer every 10 days.

✿ Propagation: Either buy plants in late spring or early summer, or sow seeds in seed trays in early spring. Place in 61–64°F (16–18°C).

OTHER FLOWERING POTTED PLANTS

Begonia—Elatior types (Elatior Begonias, Hiemalis Begonias, Large-Flowered Winter Begonias): properly known as hybrids between *Begonia socotrana* and *Begonia* x *tuberhybrida*, these are similar to the Lorraine types, but with larger flowers, up to 2in (5cm) wide. Colors include yellow, white, pink, and salmon-orange, in single- and double-flowered forms.

Begonia— Lorraine types (Lorraine Begonias): properly known as hybrids between *Begonia socotrana* (Grape-Leaf Begonia) and *Begonia dregei* (Maple-Leaf Begonia), these floriferous plants have round, mid-green leaves about 3in (7.5cm) across and masses of deep-pink flowers, 1in (25mm) wide, during mid- and late winter. Several cultivars. Colors include salmon-orange, white, deep orange, and yellow.

Begonia semperflorens (Wax Begonia): bushy and floriferous plant grown as a half-hardy annual in temperate climates and planted into flowerbeds. Colors from white, through pink and red, to scarlet during summer.

Browallia speciosa (Bush Violet): small, bushy, tender plant, grown as a half-hardy annual, with tubular, violet-shaped flowers from early summer to early autumn.

Catharanthus roseus (Madagascar Periwinkle): earlier known as *Vinca rosea*, this evergreen sub-shrub bears white, lavender, or rose flowers with darker-colored throats throughout summer and into early autumn.

Chrysanthemum frutescens (Marguerite): now properly known as *Argyranthemum frutescens*, this perennial sub-shrubby plant has branching stems and gray-green, fern-like leaves. Single, white or pale-yellow flowers, about 2in (5cm) wide, appear throughout summer.

Chrysanthemum

Chrysanthemum x morifolium (Pot Chrysanthemum): now often known as *Dendranthema* x *grandiflorum*, this is a popular houseplant with dark-green, lobed leaves up to 5in (13cm) long. Single or double flowers, 2–4in wide (5–10cm), on plants about 12in (30cm) high.

Gerbera jamesonii (Barberton Daisy, Transvaal Daisy): large, daisy-like flowers from early to late summer. Mid-green leaves, 6in (15cm) long, are deeply lobed and woolly beneath. Single- and double-flowered forms in many colors, including yellow, orange, pink, red, and white. The center of each flower forms a large yellow disc.

Begonia—Elatior type

CACTI AND OTHER SUCCULENTS

CACTI AND SUCCULENTS ARE USUALLY GROUPED TOGETHER, BUT THEY ARE BOTANICALLY DIFFERENT. ALL CACTI, WITH THE EXCEPTION OF *PERESKIAS*, ARE SUCCULENTS, BUT NOT ALL SUCCULENTS ARE CACTI. CACTI BELONG EXCLUSIVELY TO THE *CACTACEAE* FAMILY AND ARE CHARACTERIZED BY HAVING AREOLES (LIKE SMALL PINCUSHIONS) FROM WHICH SPINES, SHORT HOOKS, OR WOOLLY HAIRS GROW. MOST CACTI ARE NATIVE TO DRY REGIONS, BUT A FEW LIVE IN THE BRANCHES OF TREES IN FORESTS. BOTH CACTI AND OTHER SUCCULENTS ARE POPULAR INDOORS, AND MANY BEAR FLOWERS.

WHEN SHOULD YOU REPOT CACTI AND OTHER SUCCULENTS? THIS IS USUALLY DONE IN LATE SPRING OR EARLY SUMMER BUT THE FREQUENCY DEPENDS ON THE STAGE AND SPEED OF GROWTH OF THE PLANT. ALTHOUGH REPOTTING IS REQUIRED ANNUALLY WHEN YOUNG, LATER IT IS ONLY NECESSARY WHEN ROOTS FILL THE POT, WHICH CAN BE EVERY 2–3 YEARS. EVEN THEN, REPOT ONLY IF ESSENTIAL AND INTO AN ONLY SLIGHTLY LARGER POT. INDEED, MOST CACTI GROW QUITE WELL IN SMALL POTS. WITH SUCCULENTS, USE A SHALLOW POT RATHER THAN A DEEP ONE.

Thread Agave
Agave filifera

This succulent has white threads along the edges of its tapering dark-green, leathery leaves, which are 1in (25mm) wide. Eventually (though seldom seen on houseplants), it develops a long flower spike of purple and green bell-like flowers.

↕ **Height:** 9–15in (23–38cm)

❄ **Winter:** 45–50°F (7–10°C). Full sun

↔ **Spread:** 9–18in (23–45cm)

☀ **Summer:** 50–61°F (10–16°C). Full sun, or direct light without full sun

❤ **Care:** In winter, keep compost slightly moist; in summer, water freely. From spring to late summer, feed every 2 weeks with weak liquid fertilizer.

✿ **Propagation:** Remove offsets in spring, allow to dry for a few days, then transfer to small pots. Place in 59°F (15°C), lightly shading until established.

Queen Victoria's Agave, Royal Agave
Agave victoriae-reginae

This succulent plant has a rosette of dark-green leaves, 6in (15cm) long, with irregular white markings. Each leaf is tipped with a spine. Plants do not bloom until at least 10 years old, and then with cream flowers on tall stems.

↕ **Height:** 5–9in (13–23cm)

↔ **Spread:** 5–8in (13–20cm)

❋ **Winter:** 50°F (10°C); it survives temperatures down to 41°F (5°C) if compost is kept dry. Full sun

✹ **Summer:** 50–64°F (10–18°C). Full sun, or direct light without full sun

❤ **Care:** In winter, keep compost barely moist; in summer, water more freely and feed every 2–3 weeks with weak liquid fertilizer.

✿ **Propagation:** Sow seeds in spring and place in 70°F (21°C).

Kanniedood Aloe, Partridge-Breasted Aloe, Partridge-Breasted Pheasant's Wings, Pheasant's Wings, Tiger Aloe
Aloe variegata

Succulent plant with dark-green leaves, irregularly cross-banded, and blotched white. The stiff, keeled, somewhat triangular leaves arise in overlapping ranks. During summer, the plant develops orange flowers on stems about 10in (25cm) long.

↕ **Height:** 4–6in (10–15cm)

↔ **Spread:** 4–6in (10–15cm)

❋ **Winter:** 41–45°F (5–7°C). Full sun

✹ **Summer:** 45–55°F (7–13°C). Full sun, or direct light without full sun

❤ **Care:** In winter, keep compost slightly damp; in summer, water more freely, but allow to become slightly dry between applications. From mid-spring to late summer, feed every 2–3 weeks with weak liquid fertilizer.

✿ **Propagation:** Remove offsets in late spring; leave to dry for a few days, then repot into small pots. Place in 70–75°F (21–24°C).

Rat's Tail Cactus, Rattail Cactus
Aporocactus flagelliformis

Forest cactus with long, spine-clad, mid-green stems, ½in (12mm) wide and up to 3ft (90cm) long. It bears funnel-shaped, magenta flowers during mid- and late spring.

↕ **Height:** 2–3in (5–7.5cm)

↔ **Spread:** 2–3in (5–7.5cm), then trailing 2 ½ft (75cm) or more

❄ **Winter:** 45°F (7°C). Full sun

☀ **Summer:** 50–64°F (10–18°C). Direct light without full sun

❤ **Care:** In winter, keep compost slightly moist; in early spring, increase the amount of water. Feed every 2 weeks from when buds reveal color to the onset of late summer. Repot plants after their flowers fade—usually every year.

✿ **Propagation:** Take 3in (7.5cm) cuttings in early and midsummer. Allow the stem ends to dry, insert in sandy compost and place in 70°F (21°C).

Sand Dollar, Sand Dollar Cactus, Sea Urchin Cactus, Silver Dollar
Astrophytum asterias

Cactus with a gray-green, flattened, hemisphere-like body covered with white spots and revealing 8 spineless ribs. During early and midsummer it produces pale, shiny yellow flowers.

↕ **Height:** 1–1 1/4in (25–30mm)

↔ **Spread:** 2–3in (5–7.5cm)

❄ **Winter:** 41–50°F (5–10°C). Full sun

☀ **Summer:** 50–70°F (10–21°C). Full sun, or direct light without full sun

❤ **Care:** In winter, keep compost dry; in summer, water whenever it becomes dry. Feed every 2 weeks from when buds show color to late summer.

✿ **Propagation:** Sow seeds in spring, in 75–80°F (24–27°C).

Goat's Horn Cactus
Astrophytum capricorne

Initially, this cactus has a globular body, later cylindrical. It is light green, with 7–8 prominent ribs from which brownish-black, curved spines develop. The body is dappled with white, flaky scales. From early to midsummer, it produces yellow flowers, 2in (5cm) wide, with reddish centers.

↕ **Height:** 6–10in (15–25cm)

↔ **Spread:** 3–5in (7.5–13cm)

❄ **Winter:** 41–50°F (5–10°C). Full sun

☀ **Summer:** 50–70°F (10–21°C). Full sun, or direct light without full sun

♥ **Care:** In winter, keep compost dry; in summer, water whenever it becomes dry. Feed every 2 weeks from when buds show color to late summer.

❀ **Propagation:** Sow seeds in spring, in 75–80°F (24–27°C).

Bishop's Cap Cactus, Bishop's Hood, Monk's-Hood
Astrophytum myriostigma

When young, this cactus has a globular body, later cylindrical. It is dark green, almost gray, with silvery scales and 5–6 prominent ribs running up its body. During early and midsummer it bears sweet-scented yellow flowers up to 1 ½in (36mm) wide.

↕ **Height:** 6–8in (15–20cm)

↔ **Spread:** 6–8in (15–20cm)

❄ **Winter:** 41–50°F (5–10°C). Full sun

☀ **Summer:** 50–70°F (10–21°C). Full sun, or direct light without full sun

♥ **Care:** In winter, keep compost relatively dry; in summer, water more freely. Feed every 2 weeks from when buds show color to late summer.

❀ **Propagation:** Sow seeds in spring, in 75–80°F (24–27°C).

Old Man Cactus
Cephalocereus senilis

This desert cactus is tall in the wild but much smaller as a houseplant. It has a pale-green body and yellow spines, completely covered by long white hairs. White flowers do not usually appear when grown indoors.

↕ **Height:** 8–24in (20–60cm) when grown indoors

✳ **Winter:** 45–50°F (7–10°C). Full sun

↔ **Spread:** 3–6in (7.5–15cm) when grown indoors

✴ **Summer:** 50–75°F (10–24°C). Full sun, or direct light without full sun

❤ **Care:** In winter, keep compost barely moist; in summer, water freely and feed every 2 weeks.

❀ **Propagation:** As it ages, the lower part becomes unattractive; cut off the top, allow the cut to dry for a few days, then insert in sandy compost, preferably in spring or summer, and place in 59–64°F (15–18°C).

Apple Cactus, Column Cactus, Peruvian Apple, Peruvian Apple Cactus
Cereus peruvianus (Cereus uruguayanus)

This columnar cactus has a bluish-green, ribbed column and stout, brown spines. Eventually, it produces large, scented, white, funnel-shaped flowers, 2–3in (5–7.5cm) wide. *Cereus peruvianus monstrosus*, sometimes listed as *Cereus* 'Monstrosus' (pictured), is an unusual form that is much smaller than the species and has attractively distorted, branched stems with irregular ribs.

↕ **Height:** 2–3ft (60–90cm) when grown indoors

✳ **Winter:** 41–45°F (5–7°C). Full sun

↔ **Spread:** 3–6in (7.5–15cm) when grown indoors

✴ **Summer:** 50–75°F (10–24°C). Full sun, or direct light without full sun

❤ **Care:** In winter, keep compost barely moist; in summer, water freely. From late spring to late summer, feed every 2 weeks with weak liquid fertilizer.

❀ **Propagation:** When plants become too large, cut off the top, allow the cut surface to dry slightly, and insert in sandy compost, preferably in spring or summer, and place in 59–64°F (15–18°C). The lower part is usually discarded.

Peanut Cactus
Chamaecereus silvestrii
(Echinopsis chamaecereus)

Desert cactus with finger-like green stems that create a sprawling plant with a profusion of brilliant scarlet flowers during spring and early summer.

↕ **Height:** 4–6in (10–15cm)

❄ **Winter:** 35–45°F (2–7°C); it survives lower temperatures, but the compost must be kept dry. Avoid high winter temperatures, which discourage flower bud formation. Full sun

↔ **Spread:** 5–6in (13–15cm), then spreading

☀ **Summer:** 50–80°F (10–27°C). Full sun, or direct light without full sun

❤ **Care:** In winter, keep compost barely moist; in summer, water freely. From late spring to late summer, feed every 2 weeks with weak liquid fertilizer.

✿ **Propagation:** Short pieces of stem can be removed in spring, inserted in sandy compost, and placed in 59–64°F (15–18°C).

Silver Torch
Cleistocactus strausii

Desert cactus with a columnar nature, densely covered in short, white spines that impart a silvery gleam. Mature specimens sometimes produce tubular, scarlet flowers, 3in (7.5cm) long, during mid- and late summer.

↕ **Height:** 3–6ft (90cm–1.8m)

❄ **Winter:** 41–50°F (5–10°C). Full sun

↔ **Spread:** 4–5in (10–13cm); sometimes forms a clump

☀ **Summer:** 50–75°F (10–24°C). Full sun

❤ **Care:** In winter, keep compost barely moist; in summer, water freely. Throughout summer, feed every 2 weeks with liquid fertilizer.

✿ **Propagation:** Sow seeds in spring and place in 70°F (21°C).

Pig's Ears
Cotyledon orbiculata

Succulent, evergreen, shrubby plant with branching stems and large, gray-green leaves, 5in (13cm) long and 2–3in (5–7.5cm) wide, with red edges. It produces tubular yellow and red flowers during midsummer.

↕ **Height:** 2–3ft (60–90cm)

↔ **Spread:** 15–24in (38–60cm)

❇ **Winter:** 50–55°F (10–13°C); survives temperatures down to 41°F (5°C) if compost is kept dry. Full sun

☀ **Summer:** 55–70°F (13–21°C). Full sun, or direct light without full sun

❤ **Care:** In winter, water sparingly, especially if temperature is low; in summer, water freely but ensure good drainage. From late spring to late summer, feed every 2 weeks with weak liquid fertilizer.

❀ **Propagation:** Remove one or two leaves in early summer, allow the cut surface to dry, and insert in sandy compost. Place in 61°F (16°C).

Moss Cypress, Princess Pine, Rattail Cypress, Toy Cypress, Watch-Chain Cypress
Crassula muscosa

Also known as *Crassula lycopodioides*, this succulent resembles a miniature cypress. It has branching stems clothed in small, fleshy, overlapping, scale-like and triangular, mid- to dark-green leaves.

↕ **Height:** 6–10in (15–25cm)

↔ **Spread:** 4–6in (10–15cm)

❇ **Winter:** 45–50°F (7–10°C). Direct light without full sun

☀ **Summer:** 50–59°F (10–15°C). Direct light without full sun

❤ **Care:** In winter, keep compost slightly moist; in summer, water more freely and feed every 2–3 weeks with weak liquid fertilizer.

❀ **Propagation:** Divide congested plants when being repotted and place in 50°F (10°C).

Airplane Plant, Airplane Propeller Plant, Propeller Plant, Scarlet Paint Brush, Sickle Plant

Crassula perfolata var. *falcata* (*Crassula falcata*)

Shrubby succulent with thickened stems and blue-green, fleshy leaves. The clusters of orange-red flowers during summer give the plant its common name: 3in (7.5cm) wide, they look like airplane propellers from above.

↕ **Height:** 15–24in (38–60cm)

↔ **Spread:** 10–12in (25–30cm)

❄ **Winter:** 45–55°F (7–13°C); it survives temperatures down to 41°F (5°C) if compost is kept relatively dry. Full sun

☀ **Summer:** 55–70°F (13–21°C). Full sun, or direct light without full sun

❤ **Care:** In winter, keep compost barely moist but do not allow it to dry out; in summer, water more freely. Feed with weak liquid fertilizer every 2 weeks from late spring to late summer.

✿ **Propagation:** Take leaf cuttings in spring, insert in sandy compost, and place in 70°F (24°C).

Baby Echeveria, Painted Lady

Echeveria derenbergii

Succulent with broad, spoon-shaped, pale-green leaves with red edges and covered with a white bloom. The leaves are tightly packed to form an attractive rosette. Later, it forms a cushion, with freely developing offsets. During midsummer, it bears orange-yellow, bell-shaped flowers on stems about 3in (7.5cm) high.

↕ **Height:** 2–3in (5–7.5cm)

↔ **Spread:** 3–5in (7.5–13cm)

❄ **Winter:** 41–45°F (5–7°C); avoid high temperatures. Full sun

☀ **Summer:** 50–70°F (10–21°C). Full sun, or direct light without full sun

❤ **Care:** In winter, keep compost slightly moist; in summer, water freely. From late spring to late summer, feed every 2 weeks with weak liquid fertilizer.

✿ **Propagation:** Take leaf cuttings in late spring and insert in sandy compost. Place in 59–64°F (15–18°C).

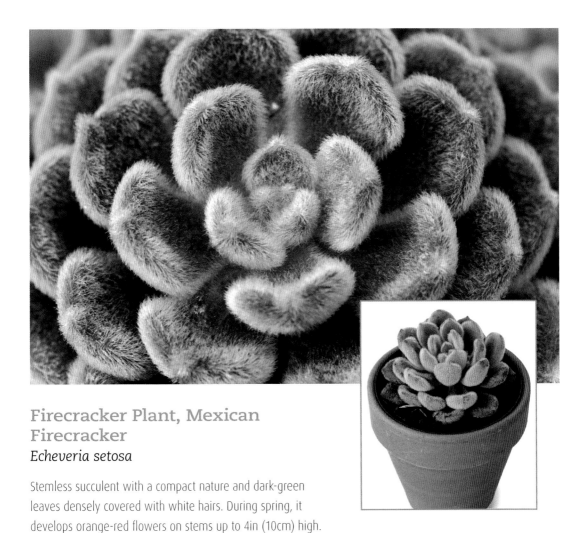

Firecracker Plant, Mexican Firecracker
Echeveria setosa

Stemless succulent with a compact nature and dark-green leaves densely covered with white hairs. During spring, it develops orange-red flowers on stems up to 4in (10cm) high.

↕ **Height:** 3–4in (7.5–10cm)

↔ **Spread:** 4–5in (10–13cm)

❄ **Winter:** 41–45°F (5–7°C); avoid high temperatures. Full sun

☀ **Summer:** 50–70°F (10–21°C). Full sun, or direct light without full sun

❤ **Care:** In winter, keep compost slightly moist; in summer, water freely. From late spring to late summer, feed every 2 weeks with weak liquid fertilizer.

✿ **Propagation:** Take leaf cuttings in late spring and insert in sandy compost. Place in 59–64°F (15–18°C).

Barrel Cactus, Golden Ball, Golden Ball Cactus, Golden Barrel Cactus
Echinocactus grusonii

A slow-growing cactus, primarily grown for its barrel-like shape, it is covered with golden-yellow, awl-shaped spines. Small, yellow flowers appear on very large plants when positioned in full sun.

‡ **Height:** 4–6in (10–15cm) as a houseplant; 3ft (90cm) or more in the wild

↔ **Spread:** 5–6in (13–15cm) as a houseplant; 12in (30cm) in the wild

❄ **Winter:** 45–50°F (7–10°C); survives temperatures down to 41°F (5°C) if compost is kept dry. Full sun

☀ **Summer:** 50–80°F (10–27°C). Full sun

❤ **Care:** In winter, keep compost barely moist; in summer, water freely whenever it becomes dry. Feed every 2 weeks from late spring to late summer with weak liquid fertilizer.

✿ **Propagation:** Sow seeds in spring in sandy compost. Place in 75°F (24°C).

Peyote Verde
Echinocereus knippelianus

This desert cactus has deep-green branching stems formed of 5 ribs, with short, bristly spines along them. Pale-pink flowers, about 2 ½in (6cm) wide, appear in clusters during spring and summer.

‡ **Height:** 3–4in (7.5–10cm)

↔ **Spread:** 2in (5cm), but then forms a clump

❄ **Winter:** 41°F (5°C). Full sun

☀ **Summer:** 50–64°F (10–18°C). Full sun

❤ **Care:** In winter, keep compost relatively dry; in summer, water freely and feed every 2 weeks with weak liquid fertilizer.

✿ **Propagation:** Sow seeds in spring, placing them in 70°F (21°C).

Cabeza del Viego,
Old Man's Cap
Echinocereus pectinatus

Desert cactus with a cylindrical nature, formed of a green stem with 25 ribs covered with clusters of small, comb-like white spines. During early summer it bears cerise-pink flowers, 3in (7.5cm) long, that open to form wide bells.

↕ **Height:** 6–8in (15–20cm)

❈ **Winter:** 41°F (5°C). Full sun

↔ **Spread:** 3in (7.5cm), branching and spreading

✳ **Summer:** 50–64°F (10–18°C). Full sun

❤ **Care:** In winter, keep compost relatively dry; in summer, water freely and feed every 2 weeks with weak liquid fertilizer.

❀ **Propagation:** Sow seeds in spring, placing them in 70°F (21°C).

Sea Urchin Cactus
Echinopsis eyriesii

This cactus is initially globular, but later elongated and branching. It has 15 prominent ribs clothed in short, dark-brown spines. It is mainly grown for its scented pure-white flowers, 6in (15cm) long, which open during summer evenings. Of many hybrids, perhaps the most popular is *Echinopsis* 'Green Gold,' with golden-yellow flowers.

↕ **Height:** 6in (15cm) or more

❈ **Winter:** 35–41°F (2–5°C); avoid high temperature to ensure the plant flowers well the following summer. Full sun

↔ **Spread:** 3–5in (7.5–13cm)

✳ **Summer:** 50–70°F (10–21°C). Full sun, or direct light without full sun

❤ **Care:** In winter, keep compost relatively dry; in summer, water freely. From late spring to late summer, feed every 2 weeks with weak liquid fertilizer.

❀ **Propagation:** Remove offsets in spring or early summer; allow cut surfaces to dry, insert in sandy compost, and place in 59–64°F (15–18°C).

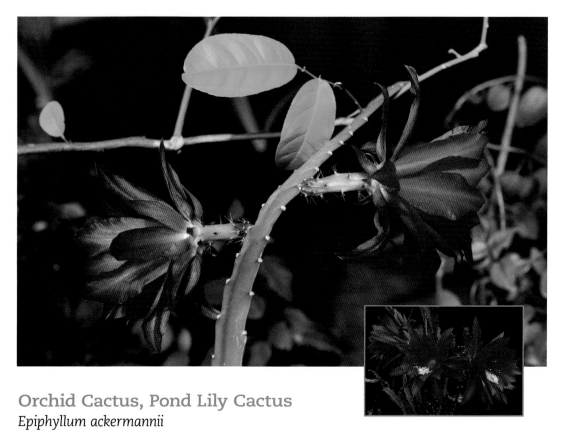

Orchid Cactus, Pond Lily Cactus
Epiphyllum ackermannii

Now known as *Nopalxochia ackermanii*, this forest cactus has leaning stems that need support when it is flowering—mainly in late spring and early summer, sometimes into midsummer. Many plants sold as *Epiphyllum ackermanii* are hybrids, which are easier to grow than the species. Hybrids are divided into two types: those with red or scarlet flowers, often 4–6in (10–15cm) wide; and those with yellow or white flowers, 4in (10cm) wide, which open during evenings (many reveal a sweet scent).

↕ **Height:** 2–3ft (60–90cm)

↔ **Spread:** 10–12in (25–30cm)

❄ **Winter:** 50°F (10°C) in early to late winter; from late winter to mid-spring, increase this to 55°F (13°C). Direct light without full sun

☀ **Summer:** 55–70°F (13–21°C); from late summer to early winter, maintain 50–55°F (10–13°C). Direct light without full sun

❤ **Care:** From early to late winter, keep compost lightly moist, never letting it dry out. From late winter to early spring, slowly increase the amount of water. From mid-spring to late summer, keep compost moist but not waterlogged. From late summer to early winter, keep compost moist, watering when it shows signs of becoming dry. From when the flower buds start to form to when the last flower fades, feed every 2 weeks with weak, high-potash liquid fertilizer. Epiphyllums flower best when slightly pot-bound, but every 3 years repot them a short while after the last flower fades.

❀ **Propagation:** During midsummer, take 5–6in (13–15cm) cuttings. Allow the cuts to dry for a few days, then insert in sandy compost, and place in 70°F (21°C).

Gingham Golf Ball, Living Baseball, Turkish Temple
Euphorbia obesa

This spineless succulent has a grayish-green body and purple patterning. It is spherical at first, later cylindrical. It produces sweet-scented, bell-shaped green flowers during summer.

‡ **Height:** 6–10in (15–25cm)

❀ **Winter:** 45–50°F (7–10°C); survives temperatures down to 41°F (5°C), but slightly higher is better. Full sun

↔ **Spread:** 5–9in (13–23cm)

✳ **Summer:** 50–70°F (10–21°C). Full sun, or direct light without full sun

❤ **Care:** In winter, keep compost barely moist; in summer, water more freely and feed every 2 weeks with weak liquid fertilizer.

✿ **Propagation:** Sow seeds in spring, placing them in 75°F (24°C).

Tiger Jaws
Faucaria tigrina

Stemless succulent with 4–5 pairs of gray-green, jaw-like leaves smothered in white dots. Each leaf has edges formed of 9–10 teeth. Golden-yellow flowers, about 2in (5cm) across, appear during summer and into early autumn.

‡ **Height:** 2–3in (5–7.5cm)

❀ **Winter:** 41–45°F (5–7°C). Full sun

↔ **Spread:** 3in (7.5cm), then forming clusters

✳ **Summer:** 50–75°F (10–24°C). Full sun, or direct light without full sun

❤ **Care:** In winter, keep compost dry; in summer, water freely but ensure good drainage, and feed every 2 weeks with weak liquid fertilizer.

✿ **Propagation:** Sow seeds in spring and place in 70°F (21°C).

Compass Barrel Cactus
Ferocactus acanthodes

Sometimes known as *Ferocactus cylindraceus*, this well-armed desert cactus has a spherical body, becoming elongated with age, with up to 23 ribs on its glaucous green body. Spines grow from raised gray, woolly areoles. The center spine of each group is long, red, and hooked. Yellow flowers, about 2in (5cm) long, only appear on mature plants.

↕ **Height:** 12–18in (30–45cm), sometimes 3ft (90cm) in a conservatory

↔ **Spread:** 4–6in (10–15cm)

❄ **Winter:** 41–45°F (5–7°C). Full sun

☀ **Summer:** 50–70°F (10–21°C). Full sun, or direct light without full sun

❤ **Care:** In winter, keep compost dry; in summer, water more frequently and feed every 2 weeks with weak liquid fertilizer.

✿ **Propagation:** Sow seeds in spring and place in 75°F (24°C).

[No common name]
Ferocactus horridus

Also known as *Ferocactus peninsulae*, this fearsome-looking, globular, glaucous green cactus has 12 ribs covered in groups of strong, reddish spines. The longest spine in each group is flattened and hooked at its tip. Yellow flowers sometimes appear during summer, but only on mature plants.

↕ **Height:** 4–5in (10–13cm)

↔ **Spread:** 4in (10cm)

❄ **Winter:** 41°F (5°C). Full sun

☀ **Summer:** 41–75°F (5–24°C). Full sun

❤ **Care:** In winter, keep compost dry; in summer, water more frequently, allowing the compost to become dry between waterings, and feed every 2 weeks with weak liquid fertilizer.

✿ **Propagation:** Sow seeds in spring and place in 75°F (24°C).

Ox Tongue,
Rice Gasteria,
Wart Gasteria, Warty Aloe
Gasteria verrucosa
(*Gasteria carinata* var. *verrucosa*)

This succulent has tapering, dark-green leaves 5–6in (13–15cm) long. They are borne in pairs, one above each other, and are smothered with white, wart-like blotches.

‡ **Height:** 5–6in (13–15cm)

❋ **Winter:** 41–50°F (5–10°C). Full sun

↔ **Spread:** 5–9in (13–23cm)

✹ **Summer:** 50–64°F (10–18°C). Full sun

❤ **Care:** In winter, keep compost barely moist, but give more water if temperature rises dramatically; in summer, water freely but ensure good drainage, and feed every 2 weeks with weak liquid fertilizer.

❀ **Propagation:** Divide congested plants when repotting in spring and place in 50°F (10°C).

Tongueleaf
Glottiphyllum linguiforme

Succulent with thick, tongue-like, shiny green leaves about 2in (5cm) long. In autumn and early winter, it bears golden-yellow flowers that open on sunny days and close at night.

‡ **Height:** 2–3in (5–7.5cm)

❋ **Winter:** 41°F (5°C). Full sun

↔ **Spread:** 3–4in (7.5–10cm)

✹ **Summer:** 45–75°F (7–24°C). Full sun, or direct light without full sun

❤ **Care:** In winter, keep compost slightly moist; in summer, water more freely, but not excessively, ensuring the compost is well drained, and feed every 2–3 weeks with weak liquid fertilizer.

❀ **Propagation:** Remove side shoots in late summer, insert in sandy, well-drained compost, and place in 59–64°F (15–18°C).

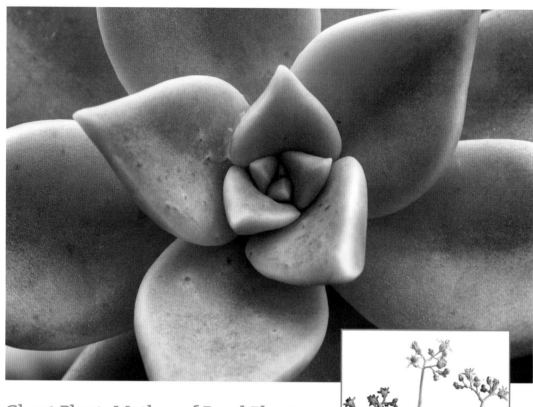

Ghost Plant, Mother-of-Pearl Plant
Graptopetalum paraguayense

This succulent looks like a miniature tree clad in short stems bearing rosettes of thick, fleshy, grayish-green leaves with a silvery bloom. At first, the stems are upright, but later prostrate.

↕ **Height:** 10–12in (25–30cm)

↔ **Spread:** 8–10in (20–25cm)

❄ **Winter:** 41–50°F (5–10°C). Full sun

☀ **Summer:** 50–80°F (10–27°C). Full sun, or direct light without full sun

❤ **Care:** In winter, keep compost just moist, but not dry; in summer, water freely and feed every 2 weeks with weak liquid fertilizer.

✿ **Propagation:** In spring, cut off rosettes (with several inches of stem), allow to dry slightly, then insert in well-drained compost, and place in 59–64°F (15–18°C).

Pearl Haworthia, Pearl Plant
Haworthia margaritifera

Earlier known as *Haworthia pumila*, this succulent forms a stemless rosette of curved, fleshy, dark-green leaves with white, wart-like protuberances. In mid- and late summer, it develops small, bell-like, greenish-white flowers at the ends of long, wiry stems.

⇕ **Height:** 3–4in (7.5–10cm)

↔ **Spread:** 5–6in (13–15cm)

❄ **Winter:** 41–50°F (5–10°C); avoid low temperatures. Full sun

✹ **Summer:** 50–70°F (10–21°C). Full sun, or direct light without full sun

❤ **Care:** In winter, keep compost barely moist, especially if temperature is low; in summer, keep compost moist but allow it to dry out between waterings, and feed every 2 weeks with weak liquid fertilizer.

✿ **Propagation:** Remove offsets in early summer, allow to dry slightly, pot into well-drained compost, and place in 59–64°F (15–18°C).

Devil's Backbone
Kalanchoe daigremontiana

Earlier known as *Bryophyllum daigremontianum*, this distinctive succulent has an unbranched central stem and fleshy, slightly triangular, green leaves about 4–6in (10–15cm) long. They are marbled with brown and curl slightly upward at their edges. The undersides are blotched with purple, and small plantlets develop along their edges.

⇕ **Height:** 2–3ft (60–90cm)

↔ **Spread:** 10–12in (25–30cm)

❄ **Winter:** 45–50°F (7–10°C). Full sun

✹ **Summer:** 50–61°F (10–16°C). Direct light without full sun

❤ **Care:** In winter, keep compost slightly moist; in summer, water more freely and feed every 2 weeks with weak liquid fertilizer. Once in a large pot, plants are usually left until they become too large, then replaced.

✿ **Propagation:** Remove small plantlets from the edges of leaves, press into compost, and place in 50–61°F (10–16°C). When rooted, transfer into separate pots.

Chandelier Plant
Kalanchoe delagoensis

Still popularly known as *Bryophyllum tubiflorum* and *Kalanchoe tubiflora*, this succulent, shrublet-like plant develops a stiff stem. The cylindrical leaves are green, blotched brown, and about 3in (7.5cm) long, with a distinctive furrow. Small plantlets develop at the ends of these leaves. In spring, small, bell-shaped, orange flowers are sometimes produced.

↕ **Height:** 1 ½–3ft (45–90cm)

❄ **Winter:** 45–50°F (7–10°C). Full sun

↔ **Spread:** 6–9in (15–23cm)

❊ **Summer:** 50–61°F (10–16°C). Direct light without full sun

❤ **Care:** In winter, keep compost slightly moist; in summer, water more freely but ensure compost is well drained, and feed every 2 weeks with weak liquid fertilizer. Once in a large pot, plants are usually left until they become too large, then replaced.

✿ **Propagation:** Remove small plantlets from the ends of leaves, press into compost, and place in 50–61°F (10–16°C). When rooted, repot into separate pots.

Panda Bear Plant, Panda Plant, Plush Plant, Pussy Ears
Kalanchoe tomentosa

This succulent has a mass of thick leaves, which, like the stems, are smothered with whitish hairs that create the impression of soft felt. The edges of the leaves become brown, especially toward their tips.

↕ **Height:** 12–18in (30–45cm)

❄ **Winter:** 50–55°F (10–13°C). Direct light without full sun

↔ **Spread:** 8–10in (20–25cm)

❊ **Summer:** 55–64°F (13–18°C). Direct light without full sun

❤ **Care:** In winter, keep compost slightly moist; in summer, water more freely and feed every 2 weeks with weak liquid fertilizer.

✿ **Propagation:** Sow seeds in spring and place in 75°F (24°C).

Flowering Stone, Living Stone, Mimicry Plant, Stoneface
Lithops pseudotruncatella

Low-growing succulent with an olive-green, rounded body and brown markings radiating from a central cleft. Yellow flowers appear in early summer. There are several popular forms.

↕ **Height:** 1 1/4in (3cm)

✽ **Winter:** 41–50°F (5–10°C). Full sun

↔ **Spread:** 1 ½in (36mm); forms clumps

✳ **Summer:** 50–80°F (10–27°C). Full sun

❤ **Care:** During winter, keep compost dry; in summer, water sparingly but do not give any water until the old leaves have shriveled (usually in late spring). Throughout summer, feed every 2 weeks with weak liquid fertilizer.

✿ **Propagation:** Divide congested clumps in spring and place in 50°F (10°C).

Powder Puff Cactus
Mammillaria bocasana

Desert cactus with rounded, dark, bluish-green cushions covered with white spines and silky hairs. During midsummer it bears bell-shaped, creamy yellow flowers, ½in (12mm) wide.

↕ **Height:** 4–6in (10–15cm)

✽ **Winter:** 41–45°F (5–7°C). Full sun

↔ **Spread:** 2in (5cm); forms a mound of rounded cushions up to 6in (15cm) wide

✳ **Summer:** 50–70°F (10–21°C). Full sun

❤ **Care:** In winter, keep compost relatively dry; in summer, water freely, ensuring the compost is well drained, and feed every 2 weeks with weak liquid fertilizer.

✿ **Propagation:** Remove offsets in early summer, allow cut ends to dry slightly, insert in sandy compost, and place in 50–61°F (10–16°C).

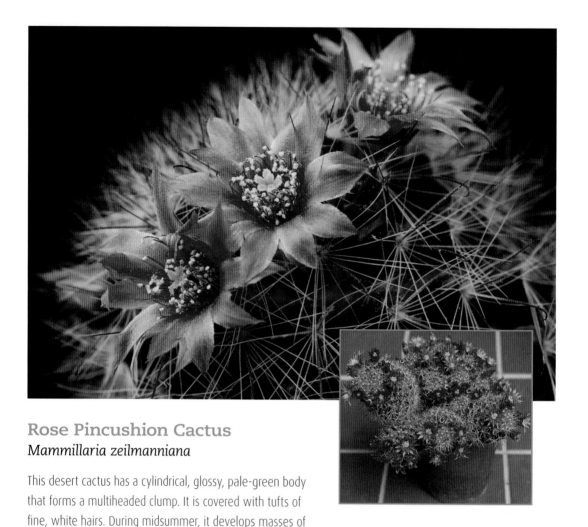

Rose Pincushion Cactus
Mammillaria zeilmanniana

This desert cactus has a cylindrical, glossy, pale-green body that forms a multiheaded clump. It is covered with tufts of fine, white hairs. During midsummer, it develops masses of reddish flowers about ¾in (18mm) wide.

↕ **Height:** 2in (5cm)

↔ **Spread:** Forms clusters

❄ **Winter:** 41–45°F (5–7°C). Full sun

☀ **Summer:** 50–70°F (10–21°C). Full sun

❤ **Care:** In winter, keep compost relatively dry; in summer, water freely but ensure the compost is well drained (do not let water rest on the cushions). Throughout summer, feed every 2 weeks with weak liquid fertilizer.

✿ **Propagation:** Remove offsets in early summer, allow cut ends to dry slightly, insert in sandy compost, and place in 50–61°F (10–16°C).

Scarlet Ball Cactus
Notocactus haselbergii

Also known as *Parodia haselbergii*, this desert cactus has a globular or cylindrical nature, with a flattened top. Its bright-green body is covered with whitish-yellow spines and 30 or more shallow, spiraling ribs. The woolly white areoles bear about 20 spines. During late spring and early summer, it produces bright orange-red flowers.

⇕ **Height:** 5–6in (13–15cm)

⬌ **Spread:** 2–3in (5–7.5cm), then spreading

❆ **Winter:** 41–50°F (5–10°C). Full sun

☀ **Summer:** 50–75°F (10–24°C). Full sun

❤ **Care:** In winter, keep compost dry, especially if temperature falls below the level indicated; in summer, water freely and feed every 2 weeks with weak liquid fertilizer.

✿ **Propagation:** Sow seeds in spring and place in 75°F (24°C).

Golden Ball Cactus
Notocactus leninghausii

Sometimes known as *Parodia leninghausii*, this slow-growing desert cactus is initially globular, but after about 3 years has a cylindrical outline. It has a pale-green body, with about 30 ribs bearing a mixture of pale- and golden-yellow spines. From early to late summer, it produces bright yellow flowers.

⇕ **Height:** 7–10in (18–25cm) in a pot, but can reach 3ft (90cm) when in a border, greenhouse, or conservatory

⬌ **Spread:** 4–5in (10–13cm)

❆ **Winter:** 41–50°F (5–10°C). Full sun

☀ **Summer:** 50–75°F (10–24°C). Full sun

❤ **Care:** In winter, keep compost dry, especially if temperature falls below the level indicated; in summer, water freely and feed every 2 weeks with weak liquid fertilizer.

✿ **Propagation:** Sow seeds in spring and place in 75°F (24°C).

Lemon Ball, Tom Thumb
Notocactus mammulosus

Also known as *Parodia mammulosa*, this easily grown desert cactus has a globular, dark-green body that is depressed and spineless at the top. It reveals 18–20 deeply notched ribs, with yellow-brown and brown-tipped spines. During most of summer, it has yellow flowers with a red stripe on the outer petals.

↕ **Height:** 4in (10cm)

↔ **Spread:** 3–7in (7.5–18cm), then spreading

❄ **Winter:** 41–50°F (5–10°C). Full sun

☀ **Summer:** 50–75°F (10–24°C). Full sun

❤ **Care:** In winter, keep compost dry, especially if the temperature falls below the level indicated; in summer, keep compost moist and feed every 2 weeks with weak liquid fertilizer.

✿ **Propagation:** Sow seeds in spring and place in 75°F (24°C).

[No common name]
Notocactus ottonis

Also known as *Parodia ottonis*, this desert cactus eventually has a clustering nature. Initially, it has a solitary, deep-green, cylindrical, or globular body with a flattened top, about 3in (7.5cm) wide, and ribs bearing slender, yellow-brown spines. Yellow flowers, up to 4in (10cm) long, appear from late spring to midsummer.

↕ **Height:** 4in (10cm)

↔ **Spread:** 3–7in (7.5–18cm)

❄ **Winter:** 41–50°F (5–10°C). Full sun

☀ **Summer:** 50–75°F (10–24°C). Full sun

❤ **Care:** In winter, keep compost dry, especially if the temperature falls below the level indicated; in summer, water freely and feed every 2 weeks with weak liquid fertilizer.

✿ **Propagation:** Sow seeds in spring and place in 75°F (24°C).

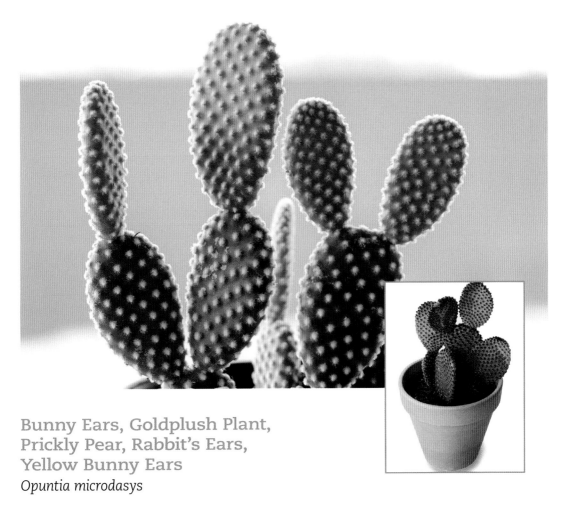

Bunny Ears, Goldplush Plant, Prickly Pear, Rabbit's Ears, Yellow Bunny Ears
Opuntia microdasys

Much-branched desert cactus with bright-green, pad-like leaves that are really flattened stems. These pads do not have spines, but are covered with attractive tufts of yellow, barbed bristles. Plants in the wild develop yellow flowers, but those indoors seldom bloom. There are several superb forms with reddish or white clusters of bristles.

↕ **Height:** 10–12in (25–30cm) when grown in a pot, but up to 3ft (90cm) in a conservatory or greenhouse

↔ **Spread:** 6–8in (15–20cm) when grown in a pot, but 12–15in (30–38cm) in a conservatory or greenhouse

❄ **Winter:** 45–55°F (7–13°C); do not allow temperature to fall below the lowest figure. Full sun

☀ **Summer:** 55–80°F (13–27°C). Full sun

❤ **Care:** In winter, keep compost slightly moist; in summer, water freely and feed every 2 weeks with weak liquid fertilizer.

✿ **Propagation:** During midsummer, remove young pads, allow cut ends to dry, insert in sandy compost, and place in 55–64°F (13–18°C).

Carrion Flower, Starfish Cactus, Toad Cactus

Orbea variegata

Also known as *Stapelia variegata*, this succulent develops gray-green stems and pale-yellow, star-like flowers in late summer and early autumn. They are 2–3in (5–7.5cm) wide, with chocolate-brown markings.

↕ **Height:** 4in (10cm)

↔ **Spread:** 6in (15cm), clump-forming

❄ **Winter:** 50°F (10°C); avoid low temperatures, which cause it to decay. Full sun

☀ **Summer:** 50–70°F (10–21°C). Full sun, or direct light without full sun

❤ **Care:** In winter, keep compost slightly moist; in summer, water more freely but avoid waterlogging, and feed every 2–3 weeks with weak liquid fertilizer.

✿ **Propagation:** Sow seeds in spring, in 64–70°F (18–21°C). Alternatively, divide congested clumps in spring and place in 64°F (18°C).

Moodstones, Moonstone Plant, Sugared Almond Plant
Pachyphytum oviferum

This small succulent has rounded, moisture-packed leaves that are covered in a silvery-white bloom and clustered around sturdy stems. During winter, the lower leaves tend to shrivel, especially if the temperature is low. In spring, it bears white, bell-like flowers on short stalks.

↕ **Height:** 6–8in (15–20cm)

↔ **Spread:** 5–6in (13–15cm)

❋ **Winter:** 41–50°F (5–10°C). Full sun

❋ **Summer:** 50–80°F (10–27°C). Full sun

❤ **Care:** In winter, keep compost barely moist; in summer, water more freely and feed every 2 weeks with weak liquid fertilizer.

❀ **Propagation:** Where a plant has lost most of its lower leaves, cut off the top rosette of leaves, plus a piece of stem. Allow the cut surface to dry slightly, insert the stem in sandy compost, and place in 59–64°F (15–18°C).

Crown Cactus
Rebutia kupperiana

Slow-growing desert cactus with a reddish-green body covered with white spines that reveal copper-colored tips. During late spring and early summer, it develops orange-red flowers, 1–1 ½in (25–36mm) wide.

↕ **Height:** 1 ½–2in (36–50mm)

↔ **Spread:** 1 ½–2in (36–50mm); eventually forms a clump 4–5in (10–13cm) wide

❋ **Winter:** 41–50°F (5–10°C). Full sun

❋ **Summer:** 50–70°F (10–21°C). Full sun

❤ **Care:** In winter, keep compost barely moist; in summer, water freely but ensure good drainage, and feed every 2 weeks with weak liquid fertilizer.

❀ **Propagation:** Sow seeds in spring, in 75°F (24°C).

Crown Cactus, Fire-Crown Cactus
Rebutia senilis

Desert cactus with a pale-green, spherical stem depressed at its top and densely covered with silvery-white, bristly spines. During spring and midsummer, it bears funnel-shaped, carmine-red flowers, ¾in (18mm) wide, with red throats.

↕ **Height:** 3–4in (7.5–10cm)

↔ **Spread:** 3in (7.5cm), but eventually forms a cushion-like clump, 10–12in (25–30cm) wide

❄ **Winter:** 41–50°F (5–10°C). Full sun

☀ **Summer:** 50–70°F (10–21°C). Direct light without full sun

❤ **Care:** In winter, keep compost barely moist; in summer, water freely but allow the compost to dry out slightly between waterings, and feed every 2 weeks with weak liquid fertilizer.

✿ **Propagation:** Sow seeds in spring and place in 75°F (24°C).

Easter Cactus
Rhipsalidopsis gaertneri

A distinctive forest cactus with many other names, including *Hatiora gaertneri*, *Epiphyllum russellianum*, and *Schlumbergera gaertneri*. This may appear to be a botanist's jamboree; if in doubt, ask for the Easter Cactus. It is often confused with the Christmas Cactus (*Schlumbergera* x *buckleyi*), but usually forms a much larger plant. Its stems, although usually flat, may have 3–5 angles and notched edges. From early to late spring, it bears bright red flowers, about 2 ½in (6cm) wide, with sharply pointed petals.

↕ **Height:** 15–18in (38–45cm)

↔ **Spread:** 2 ½–3ft (75–90cm)

❄ **Winter:** 55–61°F (13–16°C). Full sun or direct light without full sun

☀ **Summer:** 50–55°F (10–13°C). In temperate climates, plants are often put outside in summer, in partial shade

❤ **Care:** In winter, keep compost barely moist; in spring, when flower buds form, increase the amount of water and keep compost moist but not waterlogged. After the flowers fade, keep compost moist but not saturated. During summer, feed every 2 weeks with weak liquid fertilizer. Repot annually after the flowers fade.

✿ **Propagation:** Take cuttings during summer. Allow cut surfaces to dry, insert in equal parts moist peat and sharp sand, and place in 61–64°F (16–18°C).

Christmas Cactus
Schlumbergera x *buckleyi*

The naming of this forest cactus is often confused and you might see it listed as *Schlumbergera hybrida*. It is a cross between *Schlumbergera russelliana* and *Schlumbergera truncata* (Crab Cactus). It is well known for its branching, flat stems with untoothed edges and joints every 2in (5cm). Its magenta or rose-colored flowers, 2in (5cm) long and 1 1/4in (3cm) wide, appear from mid- to late winter.

↕ **Height:** 6–8in (15–20cm)

↔ **Spread:** 9–10in (23–25cm)

❅ **Winter:** 55–59°F (13–15°C). Full sun, or direct light without full sun

✳ **Summer:** In temperate climates, plants can be placed outside in partial shade; alternatively, keep at 50–55°F (10–13°C)

❤ **Care:** In autumn, keep compost barely moist, but increase the watering frequency as soon as flower buds form. When flowering, keep compost moist, but afterwards reduce watering frequency. In summer (if the plant is outdoors), keep compost evenly moist. From when flower buds form until flowers fade, feed every 10–14 days with weak liquid fertilizer. Repot annually after flowers fade.

✿ **Propagation:** Take cuttings during summer. Allow cut surfaces to dry, insert in equal parts moist peat and sharp sand, and place in 61–64°F (16–18°C).

Crab Cactus
Schlumbergera truncata

Also known as *Epiphyllum truncatum* and *Zygocactus truncatus*, this forest cactus is often confused with the Christmas Cactus (*Schlumbergera* x *buckleyi*), which also has flattened stems. In the Crab Cactus, these flattened stems are usually 2–3in (5–7.5cm) long, with deeply incised notches along their edges. They are bright green at first, later red. From early to midwinter, it bears flowers about 2–3in (5–7.5cm) long, primarily pink to deep red, but also in shades of crimson, purple, blue, and white.

⬍ **Height:** 8–12in (20–30cm)

↔ **Spread:** 12–15in (30–38cm)

❄ **Winter:** 55–59°F (13–15°C). Full sun, or direct light without full sun

☀ **Summer:** In temperate climates, plants can be placed outside in partial shade; alternatively, keep at 50–55°F (10–13°C)

❤ **Care:** In autumn, keep compost barely moist, but increase watering as soon as flower buds form. When flowering, keep compost moist, but afterwards reduce the amount. In summer (perhaps while the plant is outdoors), keep compost evenly moist. From when flower buds form until flowers fade, feed every 10–14 days with weak liquid fertilizer. Repot annually after flowers fade.

✿ **Propagation:** Take cuttings during summer. Allow cut surfaces to dry, insert in equal parts moist peat and sharp sand, and place in 61–64°F (16–18°C).

Beaver-Tail, Burro's Tail, Donkey's Tail, Horse's Tail, Lamb's Tail
Sedum morganianum

Succulent plant with thick, trailing stems packed with fleshy, pointed, gray-green leaves up to ¾in (18mm) long. They are covered with a whitish bloom and densely clustered toward the lower ends of the stems. From mid- to late summer, pale-pink flowers are borne in clusters at the ends of stems on large, mature plants.

⬍ **Height:** 1–2in (25–50mm)

↔ **Spread:** cascading for 1–2ft (30–60cm)

❄ **Winter:** 45–50°F (7–10°C); survives 41°F (5°C) for short periods if compost is kept slightly drier. Full sun

☀ **Summer:** 50–64°F (10–18°C). Full sun, or direct light without full sun

❤ **Care:** In winter, keep compost barely moist; in summer, water freely, allowing compost to dry out slightly between waterings, and feed every 2 weeks with weak liquid fertilizer.

✿ **Propagation:** Sow seeds in spring and place in 75°F (24°C).

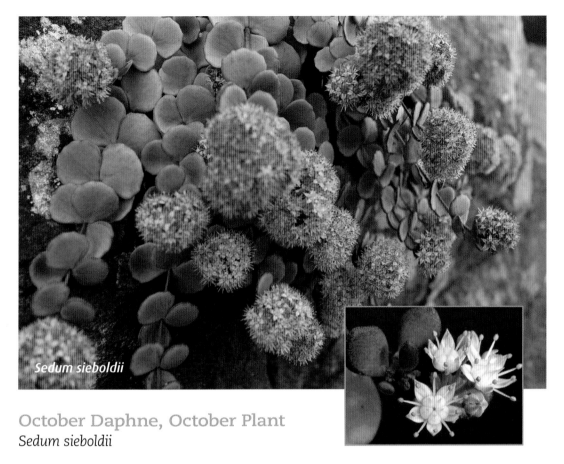

Sedum sieboldii

October Daphne, October Plant
Sedum sieboldii

Sometimes sold as *Hylotelephium sieboldii*, this succulent
plant has long, spreading stems with rounded leaves that almost encircle them. At first, they are gray-blue, but slowly change to brownish-green with a tinge of red around the edges. Clusters of pink flowers appear at the ends of the stems in early autumn. There are several variegated forms, including 'Mediovariegatum,' with slightly smaller leaves, yellow at the center, and surrounded by green.

↕ **Height:** 2–3in (5–7.5cm)

↔ **Spread:** 9–15in (23–38cm), then cascading

❄ **Winter:** 45–50°F (7–10°C); survives 41°F (5°C) for short periods if compost is kept slightly drier. Full sun

☀ **Summer:** 50–64°F (10–18°C). Full sun, or direct light without full sun

❤ **Care:** In winter, keep compost barely moist; in summer, water freely, but ensure good drainage and allow compost to become slightly dry between waterings, and feed every 2 weeks with weak liquid fertilizer.

✿ **Propagation:** Divide congested plants when repotting in spring and place in 55–59°F (13–15°C).

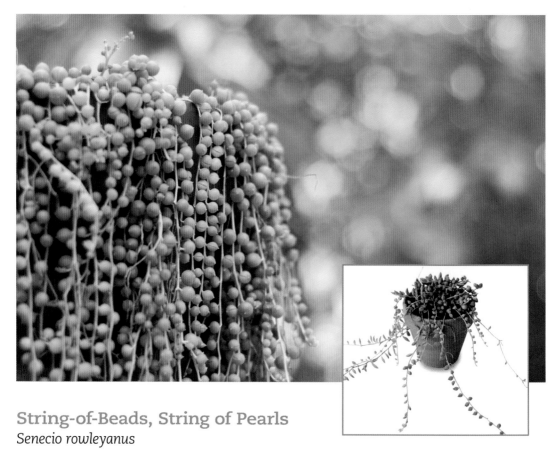

String-of-Beads, String of Pearls
Senecio rowleyanus

Trailing succulent plant with tough, wiry but fleshy stems that bear small, glossy-green, grape-like leaves. Sweet-scented white flowers with rich purple stigmas appear from late summer to early autumn.

↕ **Height:** 3in (5cm)

↔ **Spread:** Trailing for up to 3ft (90cm)

❄ **Winter:** 50–55°F (10–13°C); survives 41°F (5°C), but is happier when a few degrees higher. Full sun

☀ **Summer:** 55–64°F (13–18°C); avoid temperatures more than 70°F (21°C). Full sun, or direct light without full sun

❤ **Care:** In winter, keep compost just moist; in summer, water freely and feed every 2 weeks with weak liquid fertilizer.

✿ **Propagation:** Divide congested plants when repotting in spring and place in 55–59°F (13–15°C).

OTHER CACTI AND SUCCULENTS

Agave americana (American Aloe, Century Plant, Maguey): succulent with a rosette of thick, sword-shaped, saw-edged, gray-green leaves. 'Variegata,' with wide yellow bands along the edges of the leaves, is usually grown indoors.

Astrophytum ornatum (Star Cactus): gray, 8-ribbed, globular body, becoming cylindrical with darker markings and bands of white scales. Stout, amber-colored spines. Pale-yellow flowers appear in summer on mature plants.

Echeveria harmsii (Mexican Snowball, Red Echeveria): has a branching nature and lance-shaped succulent leaves that form large, loose rosettes. Clusters of scarlet, bell-shaped flowers with yellow tips in early summer.

Espostoa lanata (Snowball Cactus): eventually a large and tree-like cactus, but in cultivation usually 12in (30cm) high. Plants become covered with white, woolly hairs and spines.

Lithops optica (Flowering Stone, Living Stone, Stoneface Mimicry Plant): low-growing succulent with gray-green body and deep central cleft. Initially solitary, but later forms colonies. White, daisy-like flowers on short stems during late autumn and early winter.

Lobivia jajoiana (Cob Cactus): sometimes sold as *Echinopsis marsoneri*, this desert cactus has an almost cylindrical green body with short, pale red and black spines. Claret-colored, short-lived flowers with black throats, 2in (5cm) wide, in summer.

Opuntia scheeri (Prickly Pear): slow-growing desert cactus. Flattened, pad-like stems are 6in (15cm) long and 2in (5cm) wide, bluish-green, somewhat oblong ,and covered with golden spines and yellowish-brown barbed bristles.

Pachycereus marginatus (Organ Pipe Cactus): earlier known as *Lemaireocereus marginatus*, this usually forms a column with prominent ribs packed with areoles that form a white line down the plant.

Rhipsalis baccifera (Mistletoe Cactus): also known as *Rhipsalis cassutha*, this forest cactus produces pale-green stems and round, white fruits.

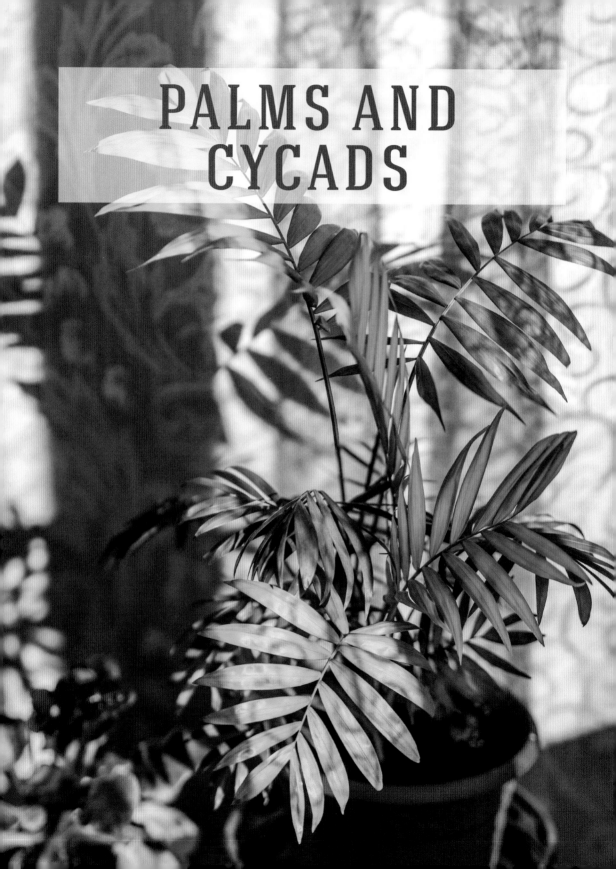

PALMS AND CYCADS

PALMS INTRODUCE A RESTFUL, STATELY AURA TO HOMES, RETAINING THEIR LEAVES THROUGHOUT THE YEAR. SOME ARE IDEAL FOR DISPLAYING ON LOW TABLES, ESPECIALLY WHEN YOUNG; OTHERS ARE MORE DRAMATIC IN CORNERS OF ROOMS OR IN CONSERVATORIES. MIST THEIR LEAVES REGULARLY, ESPECIALLY IF THE ATMOSPHERE IS DRY AND THE TEMPERATURE HIGH.

Burmese Fishtail Palm, Clustered Fishtail Palm, Fishtail Palm, Tufted Fishtail Palm
Caryota mitis

Fishtail-type palm with ragged-edged, wedge-shaped, thick, dark-green leaflets, eventually 6in (15cm) long and 4in (10cm) wide, borne on arching stems.

↕ **Height:** 5–8ft (1.5–2.4m) in a pot indoors

❄ **Winter:** 55–64°F (13–18°C). Full sun

↔ **Spread:** 2–3 ½ft (60cm–1m) in a pot indoors

☀ **Summer:** 64–70°F (18–21°C). Direct light without full sun, or indirect light

❤ **Care:** In winter, keep compost evenly moist; in summer, water moderately without continually saturating the compost, and feed every 3–4 weeks with weak liquid fertilizer. Repot in spring when roots fill the pot, though this vigorous palm is best restricted to a small pot. If in a large pot, do not repot but replace some of the soil with fresh compost.

✿ **Propagation:** In spring, remove basal suckers, transfer to individual pots, and place in 64°F (18°C).

Good-Luck Palm, Parlour Palm
Chamaedorea elegans

Feather-type palm, earlier known as *Neanthe bella*, often sold when about 6in (15cm) high, in a group of palms in a large container. Later, it can be repotted into a large pot. It produces mid- to dark-green, fairly wide leaflets on arching stems.

↕ **Height:** 1 ½–4ft (45cm–1.2m)

↔ **Spread:** 1 ½–2 ½ft (45–75cm)

❁ **Winter:** 50–55°F (10–13°C). Direct light without full sun

❋ **Summer:** 55–64°F (13–18°C). Indirect light or light shade

❤ **Care:** In winter, keep compost barely moist; in summer, provide more water but ensure good drainage, and feed every 4 weeks with weak liquid fertilizer. Repot in spring only when the compost is congested—it dislikes root disturbance.

✿ **Propagation:** Sow seeds in spring, place in 75–80°F (24–27°C).

Bamboo Palm
Chamaedorea erumpens

This cane-type palm has clusters of stems arising from compost level and bearing fronds with 15 deep-green leaflets.

↕ **Height:** 5–10ft (1.5–3m)

↔ **Spread:** 2 ½–4ft (75cm–1.2m)

❁ **Winter:** 50–55°F (10–13°C). Direct light without full sun, or indirect light

❋ **Summer:** 55–64°F (13–18°C). Indirect light or light shade

❤ **Care:** In winter, keep compost barely moist; in summer, provide more water but ensure good drainage, and feed every 4 weeks with weak liquid fertilizer. Repot in spring but only when the compost is congested—it dislikes root disturbance.

✿ **Propagation:** Divide congested plants in spring and place in 55–59°F (13–15°C).

Dwarf Fan Palm, European Fan Palm, European Palm, Mediterranean Fan Palm
Chamaerops humilis

This fan-type palm, normally tufted but occasionally with a trunk, grows 30ft (9m) high in its native area. It develops fans of gray-green segments, forming leaves up to 1 ½ft (45cm) long and 1ft (30cm) across, borne on coarse-toothed leafstalks.

↕ **Height:** 3–5ft (90cm–1.5m)

❋ **Winter:** 41–45°F (5–7°C). Full sun

↔ **Spread:** 3–5ft (90cm–1.5m)

❉ **Summer:** 45–61°F (7–16°C). Full sun, or direct light without full sun

❤ **Care:** In winter, keep compost lightly moist; in summer, water freely but ensure it does not become waterlogged, and feed every 4 weeks with weak liquid fertilizer. Repot in spring when roots fill the pot, usually every 2–3 years.

✿ **Propagation:** In spring, remove suckers from around the base, transfer to individual pots, and place in 50–55°F (10–13°C).

Areca Palm, Butterfly Palm, Cane Palm, Feather Palm, Golden Cane Palm, Yellow Palm
Chrysalidocarpus lutescens

Now known as *Dypsis lutescens* and earlier as *Areca lutescens*, this palm develops cane-like stems and feather-like clusters of yellowish-green leaflets. The fronds, 3ft (90cm) long, are on canes that gently arch.

↕ **Height:** 5–10ft (1.5–3m)

❋ **Winter:** 55–61°F (13–16°C). Indirect light

↔ **Spread:** 3–5ft (90cm–1.5m)

❉ **Summer:** 61–80°F (16–27°C). Indirect light or light shade

❤ **Care:** In winter, keep compost slightly moist but do not allow to become dry; in summer, water freely and feed with weak liquid fertilizer every 4 weeks. Repot in spring when roots fill the pot, usually every 2–3 years. When large, replace some of the surface soil with fresh compost rather than repotting.

✿ **Propagation:** Divide congested plants in spring, or remove and pot sucker-like growths and place in 61–64°F (16–18°C).

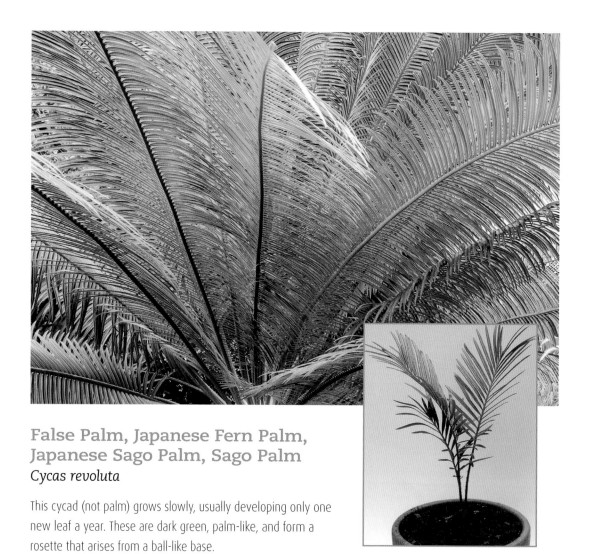

False Palm, Japanese Fern Palm, Japanese Sago Palm, Sago Palm
Cycas revoluta

This cycad (not palm) grows slowly, usually developing only one new leaf a year. These are dark green, palm-like, and form a rosette that arises from a ball-like base.

↕ **Height:** 12–24in (30–60cm), sometimes more

↔ **Spread:** 15–24in (38–60cm), sometimes more

❄ **Winter:** 59–64°F (15–18°C). Indirect light

☀ **Summer:** 64–80°F (18–27°C). Indirect light or light shade

❤ **Care:** In winter, keep compost barely moist, especially if temperature is low; in summer, water freely but ensure good drainage, and feed with weak liquid fertilizer every 6 weeks. Repot in spring when roots fill the pot, usually every 3–4 years.

✿ **Propagation:** Remove offsets in early summer and transfer to individual pots, or sow seeds in spring in compost with a temperature of about 80°F (27°C).

Belmore Sentry Palm, Curly Palm, Sentry Palm
Howea belmoreana

Earlier known as *Howeia belmoreana* and *Kentia belmoreana*, this feather-type palm eventually for a large, dominant feature. It develops large, grace arching fronds up to 1ft (30cm) wide and 1 ½ft (45cm) long.

↕ **Height:** 6–10ft (1.8–3m)

↔ **Spread:** 5–8ft (1.5–2.4m)

❄ **Winter:** 50–54°F (10–12°C). Full sun, or direct light without full sun

☀ **Summer:** 59–70°F (15–21°C). Indirect light or light shade

❤ **Care:** In winter, keep compost barely moist; in summer, water freely but ensure good drainage, and feed every 3 weeks with weak liquid fertilizer. Repot in spring when roots fill the pot, usually every 2–3 years.

✿ **Propagation:** Sow seeds in spring; place in 80°F (27°C).

Kentia Palm, Paradise Palm, Sentry Palm, Thatch Leaf Palm, Thatch Palm
Howea forsteriana

Earlier known as *Howeia forsteriana* and *Kentia forsteriana*, this feather-type palm has large, wide, deep-green leaflets. It grows more rapidly than *Howea belmoreana* and its stems are less arching.

↕ **Height:** 6–10ft (1.8–3m)

↔ **Spread:** 5–8ft (1.5–2.4m)

❄ **Winter:** 50–54°F (10–12°C). Full sun, or direct light without full sun

☀ **Summer:** 59–70°F (15–21°C). Indirect light or light shade

❤ **Care:** In winter, keep compost barely moist; in summer, water freely but ensure good drainage, and feed every 3 weeks with weak liquid fertilizer. Repot in spring when roots fill the pot, usually every 2–3 years.

✿ **Propagation:** Sow seeds in spring and place in 80°F (27°C).

Chinese Fan Palm, Chinese Fountain Palm, Fan Palm
Livistona chinensis

This fan-type palm has a slow-growing nature when indoors, forming large, bright-green, segmented fans with drooping tips.

↕ Height: 4–10ft (1.2–3m)

↔ Spread: 2–3 ½ft (60cm–1m)

❄ Winter: 45–59°F (7–15°C). Full light, or indirect light without full sun

✳ Summer: 59–75°F (15–24°C). Indirect light, especially when young

♥ Care: In winter, keep compost just moist but ensure it does not dry out; in summer, water freely but ensure good drainage, and feed every 3–4 weeks with weak liquid fertilizer. Repot in spring when roots fill the pot, usually every 2–3 years.

✿ Propagation: Sow seeds in spring and place in 75–80°F (24–27°C).

Dwarf Coconut Palm, Weddel Palm
Lytocaryum weddellianum

Earlier known as *Microcoelum weddellianum*, *Syagrus weddelliana* and *Cocos weddelliana*, this feather-type palm has a diminutive nature, only reaching 5–6ft (1.5–1.8m) high, even after 15 years. It is claimed to be one of the prettiest palms, with slightly arching fronds bearing narrow, mid- to dark-green leaflets.

↕ Height: 9–15in (23–38cm) during its early years

↔ Spread: 9–12in (23–30cm) during its early years

❄ Winter: 61–64°F (16–18°C). Full sun, or direct light without full sun

✳ Summer: 64–75°F (18–24°C). Indirect light or light shade

♥ Care: In winter, keep compost barely moist; in summer, water freely but ensure good drainage, and feed every 3 weeks with weak liquid fertilizer. Repot in spring when roots fill the pot, usually every 3 years.

✿ Propagation: Sow seeds in spring and place in 75–80°F (24–27°C).

Canary Date Palm, Canary Island Date, Canary Palm
Phoenix canariensis

This feather-type palm has arching stems bearing stiff, straight, narrow leaflets.

‡ **Height:** 4–6ft (1.2–1.8m)

↔ **Spread:** 3–5ft (90cm–1.5m)

❊ **Winter:** 45–55°F (7–13°C). Full sun, or direct light without full sun

✳ **Summer:** 55–70°F (13–21°C). Indirect light or light shade

❤ **Care:** In winter, keep compost barely moist, not allowing it to dry out; in summer, water freely but ensure good drainage, and feed every 3 weeks with weak liquid fertilizer. Repot in spring when roots fill the pot, usually every 2–3 years.

✿ **Propagation:** Sow seeds in spring and place in 64–70°F (18–21°C).

Miniature Date Palm, Pygmy Date Palm, Roebelin Palm
Phoenix roebelenii

This almost stemless, feather-type palm has dark-green leaves formed of many narrow leaflets. These create a crown of arching fronds that hang down at their tips.

‡ **Height:** 3–4ft (90cm–1.2m)

↔ **Spread:** 2–3ft (60–90cm)

❊ **Winter:** 50–55°F (10–13°C). Full sun, or direct light without full sun

✳ **Summer:** 55–70°F (13–21°C). Indirect light or light shade

❤ **Care:** In winter, keep compost barely moist, not allowing it to dry out; in summer, water freely but ensure good drainage, and feed every 3 weeks with weak liquid fertilizer. Repot in spring when roots fill the pot, usually every 2–3 years.

✿ **Propagation:** Sow seeds in spring and place in 64–70°F (18–21°C).

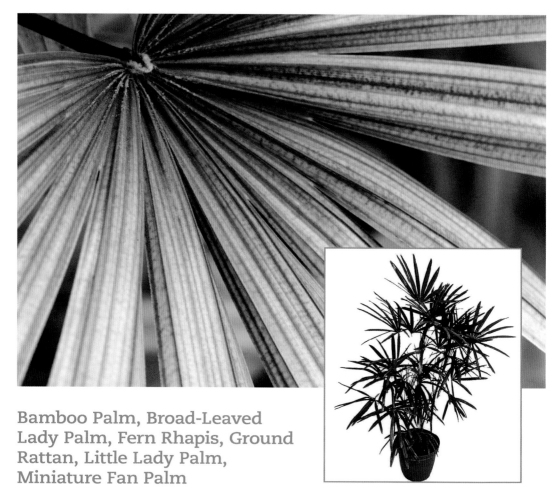

Bamboo Palm, Broad-Leaved Lady Palm, Fern Rhapis, Ground Rattan, Little Lady Palm, Miniature Fan Palm

Rhapis excelsa

Clump-forming, fan-type palm with bamboo-like stems and mid- to dark-green, finger-like leaves radiating from their tops like a fan. Each leaf is about 8in (20cm) long.

⇕ **Height:** 3–5ft (90cm–1.5m)

↔ **Spread:** 2 ½–3ft (75–90cm)

❄ **Winter:** 55–59°F (13–15°C). Direct light without full sun, or indirect light

☀ **Summer:** 61–70°F (16–21°C). Indirect light or light shade

❤ **Care:** In winter, keep compost just moist; in summer, water freely but ensure good drainage, and feed with weak liquid fertilizer every 3 weeks. Repot in spring when roots fill the pot, usually every 2–3 years.

✿ **Propagation:** In early summer, remove and transfer suckers to small pots and place in 61–64°F (16–18°C).

Chamaedorea seifrizii

OTHER INDOOR PALMS

Caryota urens (Wine Fishtail Palm): triangular leaflets on a palm with a sparse nature.

Chamaedorea seifrizii (Reed Palm): cane-type palm with deep-green, narrow leaflets.

Cocos nucifera (Coconut Palm): young plants with several leaflets often sold growing in a pot, with a coconut at the base.

Washingtonia filifera (Californian Fan Palm): fast-growing palm, eventually forming a dominant feature. It is usually short-lived indoors when grown as a houseplant, but is well worth growing, with brilliant green leaves displayed in large fans.

Washingtonia robusta (Mexican Fan Palm, Thread Palm): fan-like, with deep-green leaves.

BULBS

BULBS, SUCH AS DAFFODILS, TULIPS, AND HYACINTHS, ARE NATURE'S POWERHOUSES OF STORED ENERGY. THEY ARE FORMED OF FLESHY LEAVES ARISING FROM A BASAL PLATE AND TIGHTLY WRAPPED AROUND EACH OTHER. ALTHOUGH BOTANICALLY DIFFERENT, CORMS, TUBERS, AND RHIZOMES ARE OFTEN GROUPED WITH BULBS. CORMS ARE SWOLLEN STEM BASES (CROCUSES, FREESIAS, SPARAXIS), TUBERS ARE SWOLLEN ROOTS OR STEMS (DAHLIAS), AND RHIZOMES ARE HORIZONTAL STEMS, EITHER WHOLLY UNDERGROUND OR PARTLY ABOVE, (LILY-OF-THE-VALLEY, BEARDED IRISES).

Freesia, Florist's Freesia
Freesia hybrids

These cormous hybrids are usually grown for flowering indoors from midwinter to spring. They have fragrant, funnel-shaped flowers in a wide color range, including white, yellow, blue, orange, pink, and red.

↕ **Height:** 1 ½ft (45cm)

↔ **Spread:** 8–10in (20–25cm), when five corms are planted in a pot 5in (13cm) wide

❄ **Winter:** See below

☀ **Summer:** See below

❤ **Care:** From late summer to late autumn, plant 5 corms in a pot 5in (13cm) wide, using loam-based compost. Just cover the tops of the corms and sprinkle a 1in (25mm) layer of fine peat over the top. Initially, place in 41°F (5°C), keeping compost lightly moist. From mid-autumn, increase the amount of water; as growth begins, slowly raise the temperature to 55°F (13°C) and increase the amount of direct light. Keep compost moist while flowering; when flowers fade, reduce the amount of water and lower the temperature to 41°F (5°C). Allow the corms and compost to become completely dry. In late summer, remove the corms, store in a dry, frost-proof shed, and plant outdoors the following spring.

✿ **Propagation:** Use fresh corms each year for flowering indoors. Plants can also be raised from seeds sown in spring in 61°F (16°C). Before sowing, soak seeds in clean water for 24 hours. Germination takes up to 3 weeks.

Amaryllis
Hippeastrum hybrids

This widely grown bulbous plant should not be confused with *Amaryllis belladonna* (Belladonna Lily), a popular bulbous, autumn-flowering plant grown outdoors in warm and temperate climates. Hippeastrums mainly flower in winter and spring, but with careful timing can flower any time of year. They have green, strap-like leaves and stiff, upright stems with 3–4 funnel-shaped flowers, 3in (7.5cm) wide, in a range of single and mixed colors.

↕ **Height:** 12–15in (30–38cm)

↔ **Spread:** 8–10in (20–25cm)

❄ **Winter:** 55–61°F (13–16°C). Bright, indirect light when flowering

☀ **Summer:** 55–61°F (13–16°C). Bright, indirect light when flowering

💗 **Care:** Plant one bulb in a 5in (13cm)-wide pot, leaving half the bulb exposed. Give only a little water until growth begins, then water more freely and feed every 10 days with weak liquid fertilizer.
  · Bulbs of winter- and spring-flowering types are potted in early and mid-autumn.
  · Specially prepared bulbs for flowering in early winter are planted in late autumn.
  · For flowering during summer and early autumn, plant in early spring.

✿ **Propagation:** Buy fresh bulbs each year. Alternatively, old bulbs can be restarted into growth. Gradually reduce the amount of water after plants flower and leaves turn yellow. Then, withhold water and allow compost to dry. Place in 41–45°F (5–7°C) until restarting into growth the following season.

Common Hyacinth, Dutch Hyacinth
Hyacinthus orientalis

This popular bulbous plant flowers during winter until early spring. The candle-like heads are packed with scented, wax-like flowers in a wide color range—white, yellow, pink, red, mauve, and blue.

↕ **Height:** 6–9in (15–23cm)

↔ **Spread:** 3–5in (7.5–13cm)

❄ **Winter:** When shoot tips appear above the compost's surface, place in 50°F (10°C); gradually increase to 64°F (18°C) when the flower buds show color. Direct light without full sun

☀ **Summer:** Not applicable

❤ **Care:** Usually, pots or bowls of hyacinths are bought when buds are just starting to show color. Keep compost evenly moist, increasing the amount of water as foliage and flowers develop. No feeding or repotting is necessary.

❀ **Propagation:** After flowers fade, place the pot and plants in 41–45°F (5–7°C) in a vermin-proof shed. Later, plant into a garden.

Cape Cowslip
Lachenalia aloides

Earlier known as *Lachenalia tricolor*, this bulbous plant has strap-like leaves that arch slightly at their tips. They are pale green, about 9in (23cm) long, flecked and spotted in pale purple. Nodding, tubular, bell-shaped yellow flowers with red markings and green edges appear from midwinter to early spring. Varieties include 'Aurea' (orange-yellow).

↕ **Height:** 9–12in (23–30cm)

↔ **Spread:** 9in (23cm)

❄ **Winter:** 41–55°F (7–13°C) when in flower; avoid high temperatures. Direct light without full sun

☀ **Summer:** Not applicable

❤ **Care:** Keep compost evenly moist while flowering and continue until after the foliage dies. Keep compost dry until late summer, then repot into a clean pot and fresh compost.

❀ **Propagation:** Although plants can be kept from season to season, fresh plants are usually bought each year.

Easter Lily, White Trumpet Lily
Lilium longiflorum

This bulbous plant is widely grown as a houseplant. During mid- and late summer, it produces heavily fragrant, trumpet-shaped, white flowers with golden pollen, 5–7in (13–18cm) long and 5in (13cm) across. Several other lilies are grown indoors, including *Lilium auratum* (Golden-Rayed Lily), *Lilium speciosum* (Japanese Lily), and mid-century hybrids.

↕ **Height:** 2 ½–3ft (75–90cm)   ↔ **Spread:** 8–10in (20–25cm)

❄ **Winter:** See below   ☀ **Summer:** See below

❤ **Care:** As soon as bulbs are available in autumn, pot them singly into 6–8in (15–20cm) pots, using soil-based compost. Cover the bulb's top with 1 ½–2in (36–50mm) of compost. Water the compost and place in a dark position with a temperature of about 37–41°F (3–5°C) to encourage root development. Keep compost lightly moist. When new shoots appear, move into light shade; gradually increase light and raise the temperature to 46–50°F (8–10°C)—no higher. When flowers fade, reduce to 37–41°F (3–5°C) and keep compost moist to prevent bulbs drying out.

✿ **Propagation:** Buy fresh bulbs each year. After flowering, place the pot in a cool, shaded position outdoors. Plant bulbs into a border early the following spring.

Daffodil
Narcissus

Many types of daffodils can be encouraged to flower indoors; most popular is the large-trumpet type with one flower on each stem. Suitable varieties include 'Dutch Master' (yellow), 'King Alfred' (yellow), and 'Spellbinder' (yellow and white). Bulbs specially prepared by garden centers for early flowering are essential.

‡ **Height:** 15–18in (38–45cm)

↔ **Spread:** 12in (30cm) when several bulbs are planted in a pot 7–9in (18–23cm) wide

❉ **Winter:** See below

❊ **Summer:** See below

❤ **Care:** In late summer, select a pot 7–9in (18–23cm) wide and half fill it with damp bulb-fiber or potting compost. Place bulbs close together on top, noses level with the container's rim. Pack further bulb-fiber or compost around each bulb, so the surface is ½in (12mm) below the pot's rim. Thoroughly water the potting mixture, put the pot in a black plastic bag, and place in a cool shed (37–41°F [3–5°C]). Regularly check compost is moist. Leave bulbs in the bag for 12–15 weeks, until shoots are 4in (10cm) high. Remove the bag and take bulbs indoors, slowly increasing temperature from 45°F (7°C) to 59°F (15°C). Keep compost moist.

✿ **Propagation:** Buy fresh bulbs each year.

Harlequin Flower
Sparaxis tricolor

Half-hardy in temperate climates, this cormous plant is ideal for growing indoors. Mainly the hybrids are grown. The wide color range includes shades of red, yellow and purple, white and multicolors. Flowering is during late spring and early summer, with several star-shaped, flat-faced, 6-petaled flowers, about 1 ½in (36mm) wide, on each stem.

⇕ **Height:** 12–15in (30–38cm)   ↔ **Spread:** 8–10in (20–25cm)

❄ **Winter:** See below   ✹ **Summer:** See below

❤ **Care:** In late summer or early autumn, plant 5 corms in a pot 5in (13cm) wide, using loam-based compost. Water the compost and place the pot in 37–41°F (3–5°C). In late winter or early spring, as growth begins, provide more water and gradually move the pot into 45–50°F (7–10°C), no higher. After flowering, allow compost to dry slightly.

✿ **Propagation:** Use fresh corms each year; old ones can be planted into a warm, wind-sheltered border outdoors.

Tulips
Tulipa

Tulips such as 'Single Early' and 'Double Early' types are suitable for forcing into early flower in spring indoors. 'Single Early' types have flowers, 3–5in (7.5–13cm) wide, usually with pointed buds and flowers that open flat. 'Double Early' types have flowers up to 4in (10cm) wide that resemble double-flowered peonies. The range of varieties and colors is wide, including pink, yellow, orange, red, and mixed colors. Always use specially prepared bulbs when forcing tulips into early flower.

‡ **Height:** 9–15in (23–38cm), depending on variety

↔ **Spread:** 9in (23cm) when several bulbs are planted in a pot 7–9in (18–23cm) wide

❄ **Winter:** See below

✳ **Summer:** See below

❤ **Care:** As soon as bulbs are available in late summer, select a pot 7–9in (18–23cm) wide. Fill the base with damp bulb-fiber or potting compost and place bulbs close together (but not touching) on top of it. Their noses should be below the surface of the potting mixture, which in turn is ½in (12mm) below the container's rim. Pack compost around the bulbs, then water. Put the pot in a black plastic bag and place in a cool shed (37–41°F [3–5°C]). Some 14–16 weeks later (less for specially prepared bulbs), shoots will be about 2in (5cm) high. Remove the black bag and place the pot in 7–10°F (45–50°C). Later, when the foliage is 4in (10cm) high, increase the temperature to 64°F (18°C). Throughout, keep compost moist but not waterlogged.

✿ **Propagation:** Buy fresh bulbs each year.

Scarborough Lily
Vallota speciosa

Sometimes known as *Cyrtanthus elatus*, this is ideal for growing on sunny window ledges indoors. From midsummer to early autumn, the evergreen plants produce heads packed with up to 10 bright scarlet, funnel-shaped flowers, each about 3in (7.5cm) long.

⇕ **Height:** 15–18in (38–45cm)　　　　↔ **Spread:** 10in (25cm)

❄ **Winter:** See below　　　　✳ **Summer:** See below

❤ **Care:** Pot small bulbs in 3in (7.5cm) pots; larger bulbs, up to 3in (7.5cm) wide, in 5in (13cm)-wide pots. Pot in early autumn (although spring is also possible); leave the top of each bulb protruding ½–¾in (12–18mm) above the compost, lightly water, and place in 37–41°F (3–5°C). Initially, place in light shade; as growth begins, gradually increase the amount of light to direct light but not full sun. In spring, slowly increase temperature to 50°F (10°C), water more freely, and place in direct light without full sun. In summer, place on a warm, sunny windowsill and keep compost moist.

❀ **Propagation:** Remove offsets in autumn or spring and pot into small pots. Offsets take up to 3 years to reach flowering size, until which time place in a greenhouse that is frost-free in winter and gently warm in summer.

Forest Lily
Veltheimia capensis

This bulbous plant has shiny, mid- to dark-green, wavy-edged leaves about 9in (23cm) long. Their ends curl downwards. In spring, a tall stem, 9in (23cm) or more high, bears a tapering flower head measuring about 4in (10cm). These are packed with small, bell-shaped, pale-pink flowers with greenish tips. Varieties exist in other colors.

⇕ **Height:** 10–12in (25–30cm), sometimes slightly more　　　↔ **Spread:** 8–10in (20–25cm)

❄ **Winter:** See below　　　　✳ **Summer:** See below

❤ **Care:** In early autumn, plant a bulb in a pot 3–5in (7.5–13cm) wide, using soil-based, well-drained compost. Leave the top of the bulb about 1/4in (6mm) above the compost's surface. Water the compost and place in 37–41°F (3–5°C) in light shade. Increase watering frequency once growth begins, and raise the temperature to 50–55°F (10–13°C). Position the pot in slightly stronger sunlight and keep compost moist. After flowering, allow the foliage to die back. Rest the plant; in autumn repot the bulb into fresh compost.

❀ **Propagation:** Remove offset bulbs from mature bulbs in autumn, transfer to small pots, and place in 37–41°F (3–5°C). Sometimes, small bulbs are left around the main bulb to produce a larger plant.

OTHER BULBOUS PLANTS

Eucomis comosa (Pineapple Lily): rosette-forming basal leaves and long, poker-like head packed with green flowers in late summer.

Ixia hybrids (African Corn Lily): star-shaped, 6-petaled flowers, 2in (5cm) wide, with dark centers amid narrow, sword-like leaves during early summer. Range of colors.

Ornithogalum thyrsoides (Chincherinchee): erect, somewhat cone-shaped flower heads packed with fragrant white, cream, or yellow flowers, 1in (25mm) wide, during early and midsummer.

Polianthes tuberosa (Tuberose): tall stems bearing lax heads of fragrant, pure-white flowers, 1in (25mm) wide, during summer.

Eucomis comosa

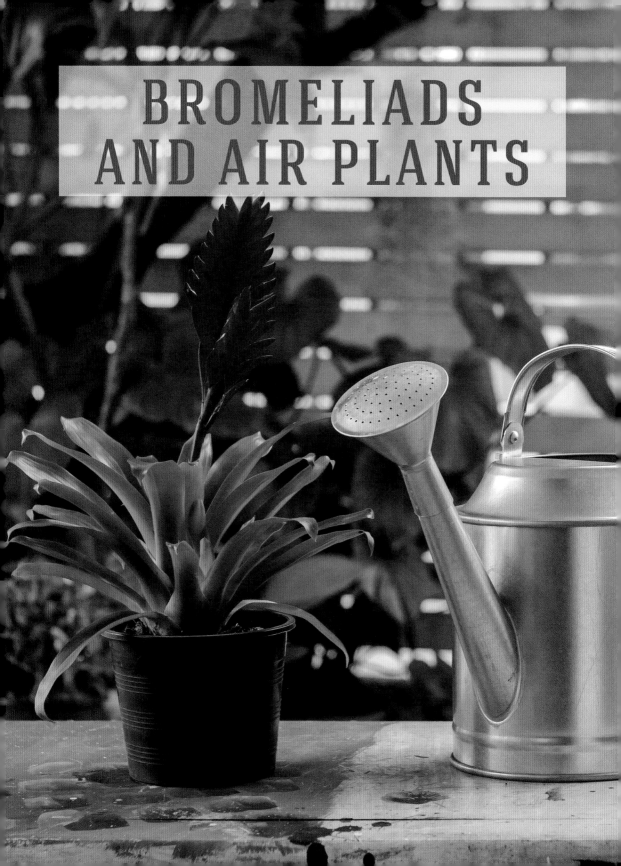

BROMELIADS AND AIR PLANTS

BROMELIADS ARE A DIVERSE GROUP OF PLANTS; SOME GROW AT GROUND LEVEL, WHILE OTHERS KNOWN AS AIR PLANTS ARE AT HOME IN TREES. SOME HAVE ATTRACTIVE FOLIAGE, OTHERS SPECTACULAR FLOWERS. A FEW HAVE BOTH QUALITIES. MANY HAVE 'URNS' AT THEIR CENTERS, THROUGH WHICH THEY CAN BE WATERED AND FED. REMEMBER TO TIP OUT OLD WATER AND REPLENISH WITH FRESH WATER EVERY 3-4 WEEKS. MIST REGULARLY AS THEY ENJOY A HUMID ATMOSPHERE.

Amazonian Zebra Plant, Urn Plant
Aechmea chantinii

This has a rosette of spine-edged and tipped green leaves, 12–15in (30–38cm) long and 2–2 ½in (5–6cm) wide. Leaves are cross-banded in silver-gray on both sides. During late summer and into autumn, orange to bright-red flowers develop.

↕ **Height:** 1 ½–2 ½ft (45–75cm)   ↔ **Spread:** 15–18in (38–45cm)

❄ **Winter:** 55–64°F (13–18°C). Indirect light   ☀ **Summer:** 64–80°F (18–27°C). Indirect light or light shade

❤ **Care:** In winter, keep compost just moist and the urn full of water; in summer, water more freely, keeping the urn full of water. From late spring to late summer, feed every 4 weeks with weak liquid fertilizer applied to the compost and in the urn.

✿ **Propagation:** Once a plant has flowered, the urn slowly dies and growth is taken over by offsets growing around it. Cut off the main plant at compost level. Once offsets are ⅓–½ the size of a full-grown parent plant, sever one close to its base with a sharp knife. Allow the cut surface to dry for 1–2 days then pot it into a clean pot with well-drained compost. Use a thin stake for support if necessary. Place in 64–70°F (18–21°C).

Silvery Vase, Urn Plant, Vase Plant
Aechmea fasciata

Grayish-green leaves cross-banded in silvery-white, up
to 20in (50cm) long and 2 ½in (6cm) wide, form an urn.
During late summer and into autumn, a stem emerges from
the urn and produces a flower head up to 6in (15cm) long.
The pale-blue flowers turn rose-colored.

↕ **Height:** 15–18in (38–45cm)   ↔ **Spread:** 15–20in (38–50cm)

❄ **Winter:** 55–59°F (13–15°C). Indirect light   ☀ **Summer:** 59–75°F (15–24°C). Indirect light to light shade

❤ **Care:** In winter, keep compost just moist and the urn full of water; in summer, water more freely, keeping the urn full of water. Feed every 4 weeks from late spring to late summer with weak fertilizer applied to the compost and in the urn.

❀ **Propagation:** Once a plant has flowered, the rosette slowly dies and growth is taken over by offsets growing around it. Cut off the main plant at compost level. Once offsets are ⅓–½ the size of a full-grown parent plant, sever one close to its base with a sharp knife. Allow the cut surface to dry for 1–2 days then pot it into a clean pot with well-drained compost. Use a thin stake for support if necessary. Place in 64–70°F (18–21°C).

Lacquered Wine Cup
Aechmea 'Foster's Favorite'

This relatively small aechmea, with sparse,
tapering, deep wine-red leaves forming a central
urn, develops a flower spike of coral petals tipped
blue in late summer.

↕ **Height:** 12–15in (30–38cm)   ↔ **Spread:** 12–18in (30–45cm)

❄ **Winter:** 55–59°F (13–15°C). Indirect light   ☀ **Summer:** 59–75°F (15–24°C). Indirect light to light shade

❤ **Care:** In winter, keep compost just moist and the urn full of water; in summer, water more freely, keeping the urn full of water. Feed every 4 weeks from late spring to late summer with weak liquid fertilizer applied to the compost and in the urn.

❀ **Propagation:** Once a plant has flowered, the rosette slowly dies and growth is taken over by offsets growing around it. Cut off the main plant at compost level. Once offsets are ⅓–½ the size of a full-grown parent plant, sever one close to its base with a sharp knife. Allow the cut surface to dry for 1–2 days then pot it into a clean pot with well-drained compost. Use a thin stake for support if necessary. Place in 64–70°F (18–21°C).

Coral Berry, Urn Plant
Aechmea fulgens

Broad, strap-like, finely spine-edged, olive-green leaves with waxy-gray undersides form a wide rosette. With age, leaves become grayish. Purplish-blue flowers appear in late summer and early autumn, followed by long-lasting, bright scarlet berries. The form 'Discolor' has leaves with purple undersides and white, powdery scales.

↕ **Height:** 10–15in (25–38cm)

↔ **Spread:** 12–15in (30–38cm)

❄ **Winter:** 55–59°F (13–15°C). Indirect light

☀ **Summer:** 59–75°F (15–24°C). Indirect light or light shade

💗 **Care:** In winter, keep compost just moist and the urn full of water; in summer, water freely, keeping the urn full of water. Feed every 4 weeks from late spring to late summer with weak fertilizer applied to the compost and in the urn.

❀ **Propagation:** Once a plant has flowered, the rosette slowly dies and growth is taken over by offsets growing around it. Cut off the main plant at compost level. Once offsets are ⅓–½ the size of a full-grown parent plant, sever one close to its base with a sharp knife. Allow the cut surface to dry for 1–2 days then pot it into a clean pot with well-drained compost, using a thin stake for support if necessary. Place in 64–70°F (18–21°C).

Common Pineapple, Edible Pineapple
Ananas comosus

Earlier known as *Ananas sativus*, this member of the Pineapple family grows 4ft (1.2m) or more high, but is usually half this height when indoors. It forms a rosette of arching, pointed, strap-like, gray-green leaves that become tinged red if in strong sunlight. The short flower stem produces blue-petaled flowers with small pink bracts. Fruits appear about 6 months after the flowers, though seldom on plants indoors. *Ananas comosus* var. *variegatus* (Variegated Pineapple), which is pictured below, is smaller, with leaves variegated green, white, yellow, and pink.

↕ **Height:** 1 ½–2 ½ft (45–75cm)

↔ **Spread:** 2–2 ½ft (60–75cm)

❄ **Winter:** 55–75°F (13–24°C). Full sun

☀ **Summer:** 59–75°F (15–24°C). Direct light without full sun

💗 **Care:** In winter, keep compost just moist and increase watering frequency as the plant becomes more active, allowing compost to dry out slightly between each application. Throughout summer, feed every 4 weeks with weak liquid fertilizer. Repot plants in spring, usually every other year.

❀ **Propagation:** During spring, sever offsets from around the base, allow cut ends to dry for a day, then transfer to compost in a pot. Place in 70°F (21°C).

Red Pineapple, Wild Pineapple
Ananas bracteatus

Also known as *Ananas sagenaria*, this slow-growing pineapple forms a rosette of leaves similar to *Ananas comosus*. It has lavender-colored flowers, followed by brownish fruits. *Ananas bracteatus striatus* (also known as *tricolor*) has leaves brightly colored in green, cream, and pink stripes.

↕ **Height:** 2–2 ½ft (60–75cm)

↔ **Spread:** 2–2 ½ft (60–75cm)

❄ **Winter:** 55–75°F (13–24°C). Full sun

☀ **Summer:** 59–75°F (15–24°C). Direct light without full sun

❤ **Care:** In winter, keep compost just moist and increase watering frequency as the plant becomes more active, allowing compost to dry out slightly between each application Throughout summer, feed every 4 weeks with weak liquid fertilizer. Repot in spring, usually every other year.

✿ **Propagation:** During spring, sever offsets from around the plant's base and allow cut ends to dry for a day, then transfer them to compost in a pot. Place in 70°F (21°C).

Angel's Tears, Friendship Plant, Queen's Tears
Billbergia nutans

Narrow, dark-green leaves and arching stems bear large pink bracts and long, tubular, green flowers edged in blue, with golden-yellow stamens.

↕ **Height:** 15–20in (38–50cm)

↔ **Spread:** 12–18in (30–45cm)

❄ **Winter:** 50–55°F (10–13°C). Full sun

☀ **Summer:** 61–75°F (16–24°C). Indirect light without full sun

❤ **Care:** In winter, allow compost to become almost dry before further watering; in summer, water more freely and feed every 3–4 weeks with weak liquid fertilizer. Repot in spring when roots fill the pot.

✿ **Propagation:** During spring, remove offsets, transfer to individual pots, and place in 64–70°F (18–21°C).

Green Earth Star, Starfish Plant
Cryptanthus acaulis

This stemless bromeliad has wavy, tooth-edged, pale- to mid-green leaves that form a low rosette. Three-petaled, scented, rather insignificant white flowers appear at any time of year, but it is invariably grown for its attractive leaves. The larger form *argenteus* is peppered with silvery scales, while *ruber* (sometimes 'Rubra') has a purple-brown shade over the green. *Roseo-pictus*'s leaves are longitudinally striped in several colors.

↕ **Height:** 2–3in (5–7.5cm)

↔ **Spread:** 3–5in (7.5–13cm)

❄ **Winter:** 61–68°F (16–20°C). Full sun, or direct light without full sun

☀ **Summer:** 70–80°F (21–27°C). Full sun, or direct light without full sun

❤ **Care:** In winter, keep compost barely moist; in summer, water more freely, ensuring compost is well-drained, and feed every 5–6 weeks with weak liquid fertilizer. Repot in spring when roots fill the pot.

✿ **Propagation:** In spring or early summer, remove offsets, transfer to individual pots, and place in 64–70°F (18–21°C).

Earth Star
Cryptanthus bivittatus

Distinctive and easily grown, this rosette-forming plant has crinkle-edged, lance-shaped, light-green leaves with dark-green stripes down the center.

↕ **Height:** 2 ½–3in (6–7.5cm)

↔ **Spread:** 6–10in (15–25cm)

❄ **Winter:** 61–68°F (16–20°C). Full sun, or direct light without full sun

☀ **Summer:** 70–80°F (21–27°C). Full sun, or direct light without full sun

❤ **Care:** In winter, keep compost barely moist; in summer, water more freely but ensure it is well drained, and feed every 5–6 weeks with weak liquid fertilizer. Repot in spring when roots fill the pot.

✿ **Propagation:** In spring or early summer, remove offsets, transfer to individual pots, and place in 64–70°F (18–21°C).

Pink Cryptanthus
Cryptanthus bromelioides

Upright, spreading plant with finely spine-edged, mid-green leaves borne on slender stalks. The form *tricolor* (known as Rainbow Star) is more colorful, with green leaves striped with creamy white lines and flushed pale pink.

↕ **Height:** 8–12in (20–30cm)

↔ **Spread:** 10–15in (25–38cm)

❄ **Winter:** 61–68°F (16–20°C). Full sun, or direct light without full sun

☀ **Summer:** 70–80°F (21–27°C). Full sun, or direct light without full sun

❤ **Care:** In winter, keep compost barely moist; in summer, water more freely but ensure good drainage, and feed every 5–6 weeks with weak liquid fertilizer. Repot in early summer when roots fill the pot.

✿ **Propagation:** In spring or early summer, remove offsets, transfer to individual pots, and place in 64–70°F (18–21°C).

Pheasant Leaf
Cryptanthus fosterianus

This spreading, rosette-forming plant has finely spine-edged, copper-brown leaves with grayish cross-banding on the upper surface. The undersides are covered with gray scales.

↕ **Height:** 2 ½–3in (6–7.5cm)

↔ **Spread:** 10–15in (20–38cm)

❄ **Winter:** 61–68°F (16–20°C). Full sun, or direct light without full sun

☀ **Summer:** 70–80°F (21–27°C). Full sun, or direct light without full sun

❤ **Care:** In winter, keep compost barely moist; in summer, water more freely but ensure good drainage, and feed every 5–6 weeks with weak liquid fertilizer. Repot in early summer when roots fill the pot.

✿ **Propagation:** In spring or early summer, remove offsets, transfer to individual pots, and place in 64–70°F (18–21°C).

Zebra Plant
Cryptanthus zonatus

Green leaves form a rosette with irregular transverse bands of green and golden-brown. There are forms, including *fuscus*, with reddish-brown leaves.

↕ **Height:** 4in (10cm)

↔ **Spread:** 6–9in (15–23cm)

❄ **Winter:** 61–68°F (16–20°C). Full sun, or direct light without full sun

☀ **Summer:** 70–80°F (21–27°C). Full sun, or direct light without full sun

❤ **Care:** In winter, keep compost barely moist; in summer, water more freely but ensure good drainage, and feed every 5–6 weeks with weak liquid fertilizer. Repot in early summer when roots fill the pot.

✿ **Propagation:** In spring or early summer, remove offsets, transfer to individual pots, and place in 64–70°F (18–21°C).

Scarlet Star
Guzmania lingulata

Shiny, bright metallic-green leaves form a rosette. During summer, a flowering stem arises from it, with large red bracts surrounded by small, yellowish-white flowers. These are short-lived, but the bracts remain for several weeks. *Guzmania lingulata minor*, known as Orange Star and sometimes sold as *Guzmania minor*, has bright orange-red bracts.

↕ **Height:** 10–12in (25–30cm)

↔ **Spread:** 15–18in (38–45cm)

❄ **Winter:** 55–64°F (13–18°C). Indirect light

☀ **Summer:** 64–80°F (18–27°C). Indirect light or light shade

❤ **Care:** In winter, keep compost barely moist and the urn topped up with water; in summer, water freely but ensure good drainage and keep the urn full. Throughout summer, feed every 4–5 weeks with weak liquid fertilizer.

✿ **Propagation:** After flowering, the rosette dies and growth is taken over by offsets around it. Cut off the old plant to 2in (5cm) of its base. In spring, remove the offsets, transfer to individual pots, and place in 70°F (21°C).

Striped Torch
Guzmania monostachya

Also known as *Guzmania monostachia*, this has narrow, green, slightly arching leaves that form a rosette. The plant develops large, poker-like flower spikes on stems about 15in (38cm) high, with small green bracts tipped with white and vertically striped in brown and purple. Toward its top, the bracts become vermilion. Only one flower stem is produced on each plant.

↕ **Height:** 12–15in (30–38cm)　　　↔ **Spread:** 15–24in (38–60cm)

✻ **Winter:** 55–64°F (13–18°C). Indirect light　　✴ **Summer:** 64–80°F (18–27°C). Light shade

♥ **Care:** In winter, keep compost barely moist, with the urn topped up with water; in summer, water freely, but ensure good drainage and keep the urn full. Throughout summer, feed every 4–5 weeks with weak liquid fertilizer.

❀ **Propagation:** After flowering, the rosette dies and growth is taken over by offsets around it. Cut off the old plant to 2in (5cm) of its base. In spring, remove the offsets, transfer to individual pots, and place in 70°F (21°C).

Blushing Bromeliad
Neoregelia carolinae

Sometimes known as *Nidularium meyendorffii*, this vase-forming bromeliad forms a wide rosette of strap-like, glossy, bright-green leaves with pointed tips. It flowers at any time of the year; flowering encourages the leaves around the rosette to turn purple or bright red. It develops small, violet-blue flowers surrounded by glossy, red bracts. There are several forms of this plant, including *tricolor*, with glossy-green leaves lined with cream and rose-pink stripes.

↕ **Height:** 9–12in (23–30cm)　　　↔ **Spread:** 15–20in (38–50cm)

✻ **Winter:** 55–59°F (13–15°C). Direct light without full sun　　✴ **Summer:** 61–80°F (16–27°C). Indirect light or light shade

♥ **Care:** In winter, keep compost just moist and the urn full of water; in summer, water the compost moderately, also topping up the water in the urn, and feed every 5 weeks with a weak liquid fertilizer. Repot young plants in spring, usually every 3–4 years.

❀ **Propagation:** In early summer, remove offsets, transfer to individual pots, and place in 70°F (21°C).

Fingernail Plant
Neoregelia spectabilis

This has narrow, shiny-green leaves with crimson tips. The upper sides often have red flecks, while the undersides are ash-gray and banded. At flowering time, the center of the plant turns rose-red, followed by a dense head of blue flowers and purple-brown bracts.

‡ **Height:** 12in (30cm)

❋ **Winter:** 55–59°F (13–15°C). Direct light without full sun

↔ **Spread:** 18–24in (45–60cm)

✳ **Summer:** 61–80°F (16–27°C). Indirect light to light shade

❤ **Care:** In winter, keep compost just moist and the urn full of water; in summer, water the compost moderately, also topping up the water in the urn, and feed every 5 weeks with weak liquid fertilizer. Repot young plants in spring, usually every 3–4 years.

✿ **Propagation:** In early summer, remove offsets, transfer to individual pots, and place in 70°F (21°C).

Blushing Bromeliad
Nidularium fulgens

Stemless bromeliad with shiny, light-green arching leaves that form an urn at their base. The impressive flower is formed of red bracts tipped with green, together with 3-petaled, violet-blue flowers.

‡ **Height:** 10–12in (25–30cm)

❋ **Winter:** 55–61°F (13–16°C). Indirect light

↔ **Spread:** 10–12in (25–30cm)

✳ **Summer:** 61–75°F (16–24°C). Indirect light or light shade

❤ **Care:** In winter, keep compost barely moist and the urn filled with water; in summer, water moderately, keeping the urn filled, and feed every 4 weeks with weak liquid fertilizer. Repot in early summer.

✿ **Propagation:** Plants are usually short-lived; once the flowers fade, the rosette dies but the offsets continue growing. Detach them in spring, transfer to individual pots, and place in 64–70°F (18–21°C).

Bird's Nest Bromeliad
Nidularium innocentii

This urn-forming bromeliad has a large rosette of finely tooth-edged, strap-like, glossy-surfaced, brownish-green leaves with metallic-purple undersides. During summer, a short stem arises from the urn, bearing 6–8 bracts surrounded by a few small, white flowers. There are several forms, including *striatum* (wide yellow stripes on the leaves and rose-red bracts) and *purpureum* (purplish-brown leaves).

↕ **Height:** 15–18in (38–45cm) ↔ **Spread:** 15–18in (38–45cm)

❄ **Winter:** 55–61°F (13–16°C). Indirect light ✹ **Summer:** 61–75°F (16–24°C). Light shade

❤ **Care:** In winter, keep compost barely moist but the urn filled with water; in summer, water moderately and keep the urn filled, and feed every 4 weeks with weak liquid fertilizer. Repot in early summer.

❀ **Propagation:** Plants are usually short-lived; once the flowers fade, the rosette dies and offsets continue growing. Detach them in spring, transfer to individual pots, and place in 64–70°F (18–21°C).

Air Plant, Pot-Bellied Tillandsia
Tillandsia circinnata

This epiphytic tillandsia gains one of its common names from the egg-like swelling (a pseudobulb) at its base. Gray leaf blades, up to 8in (20cm) long, are usually twisted, curled, or in spirals. The plant bears blue flowers with pink bracts.

↕ **Height:** 8–18in (20–45cm) ↔ **Spread:** 6–10in (15–25cm)

❄ **Winter:** 50–59°F (10–15°C). Indirect light ✹ **Summer:** 61–80°F (16–27°C). Indirect light or slight shade

❤ **Care:** These grow without the benefit of compost; plants are attached to pieces of wood, cork, or a large shell. Instead of being watered, they need to be misted regularly with clean, lime-free water. Every 3–4 weeks throughout summer, add weak liquid fertilizer to the misting water. No repotting is needed. After a rosette has flowered, it starts to die and eventually is replaced by offshoots from around its base.

❀ **Propagation:** Divide large and congested plants in spring and place in 64–70°F (18–21°C).

OTHER TILLANDSIAS

Tillandsia argentea: narrow leaves smothered in silvery-gray scales; red or green bracts and bright red petals.

Tillandsia caput-medusae: bulbous base; narrow leaves clothed in white scales; flowers formed of red, pink, and green bracts, and violet petals.

Tillandsia ionantha (Blushing Bride): stemless rosettes formed of silvery-gray, scale-like leaves. In summer, just before violet-purple flowers with yellow stamens appear, the centers of the leafy rosettes become flushed red.

Tillandsia usneoides (Spanish Moss, Old Man's Beard, Gray Beard): Often forms pendulous clusters up to 3 ½ft (1m) long from telephone poles in its native southeastern states of the United States. Tangled, wiry stems with scaly, silvery-gray leaves; bright, yellow-green flowers in summer.

Tillandsia usneoides

Pink Quill
Tillandsia cyanea

This tillandsia is grown in a pot rather than attached to a piece of wood or bark. The narrow green leaves, about 15in (38cm) long and 1in (25mm) wide, are reddish-brown at the base. During late summer, a short, central stem develops, producing a flower head of rose to red bracts, tinged green, and violet-blue flowers.

↕ **Height:** 9in (23cm)

↔ **Spread:** 12in (30cm)

❆ **Winter:** 50–59°F (10–15°C). Indirect light

✹ **Summer:** 61–80°F (16–27°C). Light shade

❤ **Care:** In winter, keep compost just moist; in summer, water freely but ensure good drainage, and feed every 3–4 weeks with weak liquid fertilizer. Repot in spring, but only when the plant is being divided.

❁ **Propagation:** Divide congested plants in spring and place in 64–70°F (18–21°C).

Blue-Flowered Torch
Tillandsia lindenii

Grown in a pot, it has dark-green, grass-like leaves, 12in (30cm) long. They arch outward and are purple on their undersides. During summer, a short, flattened head is produced, 6–8in (15–20cm) long, with pink bracts and white-throated blue flowers.

↕ **Height:** 15–20in (38–50cm)

↔ **Spread:** 12–15in (30–38cm)

❆ **Winter:** 55–59°F (13–15°C). Direct light without full sun

✹ **Summer:** 61–80°F (16–27°C). Indirect light to light shade

❤ **Care:** In winter, keep compost just moist; in summer, water the compost moderately and feed every 5 weeks with weak liquid fertilizer. Repot in spring, usually every 3–4 years.

❁ **Propagation:** In early summer, remove offsets, transfer to individual pots, and place in 64–70°F (18–21°C).

[No common name]
Vriesea fenestralis

Distinctive bromeliad, forming a large rosette of shiny, yellowish-green leaves, up to 18in (45cm) long and 2in (5cm) wide, with dark-green veins. The undersides are spotted purplish-red. During summer, it produces a flower spike up to 3ft (90cm) high, bearing tubular, rich sulfur-yellow flowers surrounded by green bracts.

↕ **Height:** 1 ½–2ft (45–60cm)

❄ **Winter:** 55–64°F (13–18°C). Indirect light

↔ **Spread:** 2–2 ½ft (60–75cm)

☀ **Summer:** 64–80°F (18–27°C). Indirect light or light shade

❤ **Care:** In winter, keep compost just moist and the urn filled with water; in summer, water more freely but ensure compost is well drained, and regularly top up the water in the urn. Feed with weak liquid fertilizer every 4–5 weeks during summer. Repot in spring, usually every 3 years.

✿ **Propagation:** In spring, remove offsets, transfer to individual pots, and place in 64–70°F (18–21°C).

[No common name]
Vriesea fosteriana

This has a large rosette of tongue-like, dark bluish-green leaves and develops a stem up to 2ft (60cm) long in summer, bearing pale-yellow flowers with reddish-brown tips.

↕ **Height:** 1 ½ft (45cm)

❄ **Winter:** 55–64°F (13–18°C). Indirect light

↔ **Spread:** 2–2 ½ft (60–75cm)

☀ **Summer:** 64–80°F (18–27°C). Indirect light or light shade

❤ **Care:** In winter, keep compost just moist and the urn filled with water; in summer, water more freely but ensure compost is well drained, and regularly top up the water in the urn. Feed every 4–5 weeks with weak liquid fertilizer during summer. Repot in spring, usually every 3 years.

✿ **Propagation:** In spring, remove offsets, transfer to individual pots, and place in 64–70°F (18–21°C).

King of the Bromeliads
Vriesea hieroglyphica

Distinctive bromeliad, with yellowish-green leaves, 2ft (60cm) long and up to 4in (10cm) wide, covered with irregular dark-purple markings. The flowering stem, often 2ft (60cm) long, arises from the plant's center and bears pale-green bracts and yellow, tubular flowers.

‡ **Height:** 20–24in (50–60cm)

❄ **Winter:** 55–64°F (13–18°C). Indirect light

↔ **Spread:** 2 ½–3ft (75–90cm)

☀ **Summer:** 64–80°F (18–27°C). Indirect light or light shade

❤ **Care:** In winter, keep compost just moist and the urn filled with water; in summer, water more freely but ensure compost is well drained, and regularly top up the water in the urn. Feed every 4–5 weeks with weak liquid fertilizer during summer. Repot in spring, usually every 3 years.

✿ **Propagation:** In spring, remove offsets, transfer to individual pots, and place in 64–70°F (18–21°C).

Flaming Sword
Vriesea splendens

This bromeliad has a rosette of sword-shaped, smooth-edged, dark-green leaves with purple-black cross-banding. In late summer, it develops a sword-like head of bright red bracts and yellow flowers.

‡ **Height:** 15–18in (38–45cm)

❄ **Winter:** 55–64°F (13–18°C). Indirect light

↔ **Spread:** 12–15in (30–38cm)

☀ **Summer:** 64–80°F (18–27°C). Indirect light or light shade

❤ **Care:** In winter, keep compost just moist and the urn filled with water; in summer, water more freely but ensure the compost is well drained, and regularly top up the water in the urn. Feed every 4–5 weeks with weak liquid fertilizer during summer. Repot in spring, usually every 3 years.

✿ **Propagation:** In spring, remove offsets, transfer to individual pots, and place in 64–70°F (18–21°C).

OTHER BROMELIADS

Aechmea blumenavii (Urn Plant): 10–15 stiff and strap-like, slightly arching green leaves, 1 ½in (36mm) wide, with scaly-white overtones and dark violet at their tops. They form a long tube. Yellow flowers in loose clusters at the tops of long, stiff stems during mid- and late summer.

Billbergia x *windii:* hybrid of *Billbergia nutans*, but smaller and less hardy, and with wider, rigid, gray-green leaves covered in gray scales (as if dusted with flour). Pendent, tubular flowers combine pink and bluish-green, with long, pale-yellow stamens.

Dyckia brevifolia (Pineapple Dyckia): shiny, green, stiff, spreading, spine-edged, tapering leaves up to 8in (20cm) long; undersides have silver lines. In late summer, flower stems arise from the plant's sides (not center) bearing bright orange flowers.

Guzmania sanguinea: urn-forming bromeliad, with broad, flattish rosette of red-tinged leaves and pale-yellow or white central area.

Guzmania sanguinea

INDOOR FERNS

FERNS INTRODUCE PERMANENCY TO DISPLAYS OF PLANTS INDOORS. THEY HAVE A LONG LIFE AND RETAIN THEIR FOLIAGE THROUGHOUT THE YEAR, SO THEY CAN BE USED AS FOCAL POINTS—PERHAPS DISPLAYED ON SPECIAL PLANT STANDS OR IN HANGING BASKETS—AS WELL AS CREATING BACKGROUND COLOR FOR OTHER PLANTS. THEY ARE NOT DIFFICULT TO GROW AND ARE IDEAL IN CONSERVATORIES, WHERE THEY CREATE A RESTFUL AMBIENCE.

Dudder Grass, Maidenhair Fern, Southern Maidenhair Fern, Venus's Hair, Venus-Hair Fern
Adiantum capillus-veneris

Perennial fern with dainty, delicate, light-green fronds on wiry black stalks.

↕ **Height:** 6–10in (15–25cm)

↔ **Spread:** 6–10in (15–25cm)

❆ **Winter:** 45–55°F (7–13°C). Indirect light

✺ **Summer:** 55–64°F (13–18°C). Light shade

❤ **Care:** In winter, keep compost slightly moist; in summer, water freely and feed every 2–3 weeks with weak liquid fertilizer. Repot in spring when roots fill the pot, usually every 2 years.

✿ **Propagation:** Divide congested plants in spring and place in 55–59°F (13–15°C).

Delta Maidenhair Fern
Adiantum raddianum

Also known as *Adiantum cuneatum*, it is more robust than *Adiantum capillus-veneris*, with long black stalks and pale-green, finely divided, triangular fronds. There are several forms, including 'Fritz Lüthi' (long, narrow fronds with overlapping, curly-edged, slightly blue leaflets) and 'Fragrantissimum' (fragrant fronds).

↕ Height: 12–18in (30–45cm)

↔ Spread: 15–24in (38–60cm)

❄ Winter: 50–55°F (10–13°C). Light shade

☀ Summer: 55–64°F (13–18°C). Light to medium shade

♥ Care: In winter, keep compost slightly moist; in summer, water freely and feed every 2–3 weeks with weak liquid fertilizer. Repot in spring when roots fill the pot, usually every 2 years.

✿ Propagation: Divide congested plants in spring and place in 55–59°F (13–15°C).

Hen-and-Chicken Fern, King and Queen Fern, Mother Fern, Mother Spleenwort, Parsley Fern
Asplenium bulbiferum

Distinctive fern with arching stems that bear mid-green, carrot-like fronds with small bulbils along their edges; they tend to weigh down the fronds.

↕ Height: 1 ½–2ft (45–60cm)

↔ Spread: 2–3ft (60–90cm)

❄ Winter: 45–50°F (7–10°C). Direct light without full sun

☀ Summer: 50–64°F (10–18°C). Indirect light or light shade

♥ Care: In winter, keep compost slightly moist; in summer, water freely and feed every 3 weeks with weak liquid fertilizer. Repot in spring when roots fill the pot, usually every year when plants are small.

✿ Propagation: In late spring and summer, remove bulbils when they show small leaves and press them into pots of equal amounts moist peat and sharp sand. Repot bulbils when rooted; place in 50°F (10°C) until established.

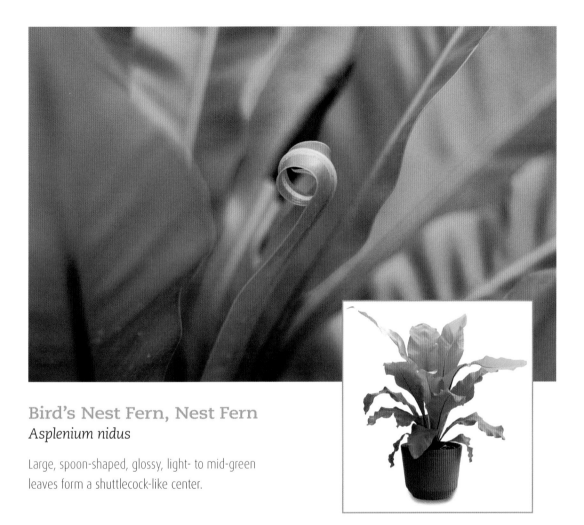

Bird's Nest Fern, Nest Fern
Asplenium nidus

Large, spoon-shaped, glossy, light- to mid-green
leaves form a shuttlecock-like center.

↕ **Height:** 1 ½–3ft (45–90cm)

↔ **Spread:** 1–2ft (30–60cm)

❄ **Winter:** 55–59°F (13–15°C). Direct light
without full sun

☀ **Summer:** 59–64°F (15–18°C). Indirect light
or light shade

❤ **Care:** In winter, keep compost just moist; in summer, water more freely and feed every 3 weeks with
weak liquid fertilizer. Repot in spring when roots fill the pot, usually every 2 years for small plants.

✿ **Propagation:** Buy plants from a houseplant nursery.

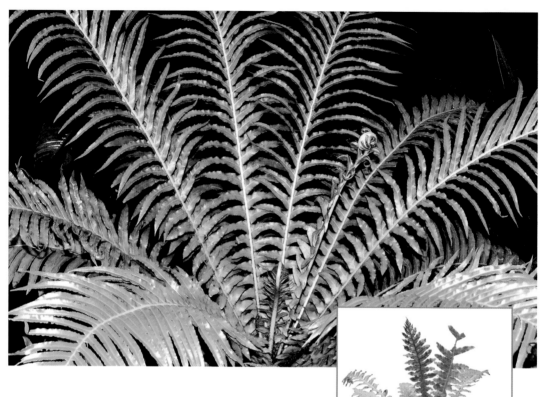

Hard Fern, Miniature Tree Fern, Rib Fern
Blechnum gibbum

Deeply cut, mid-green, stiff, crowded fronds form a spiral at the top in mature plants. Eventually, this fern forms a trunk. *Blechnum brasiliense* is another tree-like fern with large fronds and, eventually, a trunk 3ft (90cm) high.

↕ **Height:** 1 ½–2 ½ft (45–75cm)

↔ **Spread:** 1 ½–2 ½ft (45–75cm)

❉ **Winter:** 59–64°F (15–18°C). Full sun, or direct light without full sun

❇ **Summer:** 64–75°F (18–24°C). Indirect light or light shade

❤ **Care:** In winter, keep compost moist but not continually saturated; in summer, water freely but ensure good drainage, and feed every 3–4 weeks with weak liquid fertilizer. Repot in spring when roots fill the pot, usually every 3–4 years.

✿ **Propagation:** Buy a young plant from a houseplant nursery.

Holly Fern, Japanese Holly Fern
Cyrtomium falcatum

Arching fronds with stiff, holly-like, dark-green, glossy leaflets, each about 3in (7.5cm) long. The form 'Rochfordianum' has slightly larger, wavy leaflets with serrated edges.

‡ **Height:** 8–15in (20–38cm)

↔ **Spread:** 15–24in (38–60cm)

❆ **Winter:** 50–55°F (10–13°C). Direct light without full sun

✻ **Summer:** 55–64°F (13–18°C); avoid high temperatures. Indirect light or light shade

❤ **Care:** In winter, keep compost slightly moist, otherwise water freely, especially in spring and early summer when growth resumes. Feed every 3 weeks during summer with weak liquid fertilizer. Repot in spring when roots fill the pot, usually every 2–3 years.

✿ **Propagation:** Divide congested plants in spring and place in 55–59°F (13–15°C).

Deer's-Foot Fern, Hare's-Foot Fern, Squirrel's-Foot Fern
Davallia canariensis

It gains its common names from its fleshy roots covered with pale brown scales. Mid-green, leathery, somewhat triangular fronds eventually hang down.

‡ **Height:** 12–18in (30–45cm)

↔ **Spread:** 12–15in (30–38cm)

❆ **Winter:** 50–59°F (10–15°C). Direct light without full sun

✻ **Summer:** 55–70°F (13–21°C). Direct light without full sun, or indirect light

❤ **Care:** In winter, keep compost moist but not waterlogged; in summer, water freely but ensure good drainage, and feed every 4 weeks with weak liquid fertilizer. Repot in spring when roots fill the pot, usually every 2–3 years.

✿ **Propagation:** Divide congested plants in spring and place in 55–59°F (13–15°C).

Sword Fern
Nephrolepis exaltata

Ideal and resilient fern for indoors, with long, tapering, usually erect fronds and several attractive forms (see sidebar).

‡ **Height:** 1 ½–2 ½ft (45–75cm)

↔ **Spread:** 1 ½–3ft (45–90cm)

❉ **Winter:** 50–55°F (10–13°C). Direct light without full sun

✳ **Summer:** 55–64°F (13–18°C). Direct light without full sun, or indirect light

♥ **Care:** In winter, keep compost slightly moist; in summer, water freely and feed every 2–3 weeks with weak liquid fertilizer. Repot in spring when roots fill the pot, usually every 2–3 years. When already in a large pot, tease away some of the compost and repot into a same-sized pot, adding some fresh compost.

❀ **Propagation:** Divide congested plants in spring and place in 55–59°F (13–15°C).

Button Fern, New Zealand Cliff Brake
Pellaea rotundifolia

Unusual fern with small, shiny, button-like, slightly waxy, dark-green leaves along wiry stems.

‡ **Height:** 10–12in (25–30cm)

↔ **Spread:** 12–15in (30–38cm)

❉ **Winter:** 50–55°F (10–13°C). Direct light without full sun

✳ **Summer:** 55–64°F (13–18°C). Direct light without full sun, or indirect light

♥ **Care:** In winter, keep compost slightly moist; in summer, water freely but avoid waterlogging, and feed every 3 weeks with weak liquid fertilizer. Repot in spring when roots fill the pot, usually every 2–3 years.

❀ **Propagation:** Divide congested plants in spring, but not into very small pieces; place in 55–59°F (13–15°C).

ATTRACTIVE FORMS OF
NEPHROLEPIS EXALTATA (SWORD FERN)

Nephrolepis exaltata 'Bostoniensis' (Boston Fern): graceful fern, with arching fronds (wider than the species).

Nephrolepis exaltata 'Rooseveltii': distinctive and attractive, with large, wavy-edged leaflets.

Nephrolepis exaltata 'Smithii': delicate and finely divided, lace-like fronds. Has a weeping nature.

Nephrolepis exaltata 'Whitmanii' (Lace Fern): frilled, deeply cut fronds with a feather-like nature.

Deer-Tongue Fern, Hart's-Tongue Fern
Phyllitis scolopendrium

Now known as *Asplenium scolopendrium* and earlier as *Scolopendrium vulgare*, this relatively hardy fern's fronds resemble long, shiny-green tongues. Several forms have intricately shaped fronds, including 'Crispum' (edges crisped and waved) and 'Cristatum' (branched and crested tips). It is mainly the crested forms that are grown indoors.

↕ **Height:** 12–18in (30–45cm)

↔ **Spread:** 10–20in (25–50cm)

❄ **Winter:** 41–50°F (5–10°C). Indirect light

✳ **Summer:** 50–55°F (10–13°C). Light shade

❤ **Care:** In winter, keep compost barely moist; in summer, water freely but ensure good drainage, and feed every 4 weeks with weak liquid fertilizer. Repot in spring when roots fill the pot, usually every 2–3 years.

✿ **Propagation:** Divide congested plants in spring and place in 50°F (10°C).

Stag Horn Fern
Platycerium bifurcatum

Also known as *Platycerium alcicorne*, this distinctive, tender fern develops antler-like, mid-green fronds covered with minute hairs. It is best displayed attached to a piece of wood or cork secured to a wall in a conservatory, or it can be suspended. When young, it can be grown in a pot. *Platycerium grande* (Elk Horn Fern) is similar but larger and may reach 5ft (1.5m) or more wide.

↕ **Height:** 1 ½–2ft (45–60cm)

↔ **Spread:** 1 ½–2 ½ft (45–75cm)

❄ **Winter:** 45–55°F (7–13°C). Direct light without full sun, or indirect light

✳ **Summer:** 55–75°F (13–24°C). Light shade

❤ **Care:** In winter, keep compost slightly moist; in summer, water freely and feed every 4 weeks with weak liquid fertilizer. Repot in spring when roots fill the container, often annually when young but later every 2–3 years.

✿ **Propagation:** Divide congested plants in spring and place in 55–61°F (13–16°C).

Cretan Brake Fern, Ribbon Fern
Pteris cretica

Strap-shaped leaflets form light-green fronds. There are several attractive forms, including 'Albolineata' (Variegated Table Fern) with white bands along its midribs. Some have cockscomb-tipped fronds.

↕ **Height:** 12–18in (30–45cm)

↔ **Spread:** 9–15in (23–38cm)

❄ **Winter:** 45–50°F (7–10°C). Direct light without full sun, or indirect light

❋ **Summer:** 50–64°F (10–18°C). Light shade

❤ **Care:** In winter, keep compost slightly moist; in summer, water freely but ensure good drainage, and feed every 3 weeks with weak liquid fertilizer. Repot in spring when roots fill the pot, usually every 3–4 years.

❀ **Propagation:** Divide congested plants in spring and place in 50–55°F (10–13°C).

Sword Brake
Pteris ensiformis

This has slender, ribbon-like, deep green fronds. It is usually grown in the form 'Victoriae' (Silver Lace Fern, Victoria Brake Fern, and Silver-Leaf Fern), with fronds that reveal white midribs.

↕ **Height:** 15–18in (38–45cm)

↔ **Spread:** 10–12in (25–30cm)

❄ **Winter:** 55–59°F (13–15°C). Direct light without full sun, or indirect light

❋ **Summer:** 59–64°F (15–18°C). Indirect light or light shade

❤ **Care:** In winter, keep compost slightly moist; in summer, water freely but ensure good drainage, and feed every 3 weeks with weak liquid fertilizer. Repot in spring when roots fill the pot, usually every 3–4 years.

❀ **Propagation:** Divide congested plants in spring and place in 59–61°F (15–16°C).

Silvery Fern, Silvery Lace Fern, Silver Brake
Pteris quadriaurita

Usually grown in the form *Pteris quadriaurita argyraea*, also known as *Pteris biaurita argyraea* and frequently sold as *Pteris argyraea*, it has long, gray-green fronds marked with light greenish-white bands along the center.

↕ **Height:** 1–2ft (30–60cm)

↔ **Spread:** 10–24in (25–60cm)

❄ **Winter:** 55–59°F (13–15°C). Direct light without full sun, or indirect light

☀ **Summer:** 59–68°F (15–20°C). Light shade

❤ **Care:** In winter, keep compost slightly moist; in summer, water freely but ensure good drainage, and feed every 3 weeks with weak liquid fertilizer. Repot in spring when roots fill the pot, usually every 3–4 years.

❀ **Propagation:** Divide congested plants in spring and place in 59–61°F (15–16°C).

Australian Bracken, Australian Trembling Fern, Poor Man's Cibotium, Shaking Brake, Tender Brake, Turawera
Pteris tremula

This plant has slim, arching, triangular, bright-green feathery fronds.

↕ **Height:** 2–3ft (60–90cm)

↔ **Spread:** 2–2 ½ft (60–75cm)

❄ **Winter:** 45–50°F (7–10°C). Indirect light

☀ **Summer:** 50–64°F (10–18°C). Light shade

❤ **Care:** In winter, keep compost slightly moist; in summer, water freely but ensure good drainage, and feed every 4 weeks with weak liquid fertilizer. Repot in spring when roots fill the pot, usually every 3–4 years.

❀ **Propagation:** Divide congested plants in spring and place in 50°F (10°C). It often produces self-sown plants when in a greenhouse.

Didymochlaena truncatula

OTHER INDOOR FERNS

Adiantum hispidulum (Australian Maidenhair, Rose Maidenhair): distinctive, with long fronds; coppery-pink when young.

Asplenium flabellifolium (Necklace Fern): pale-green, narrow fronds; ideal for planting in indoor hanging basket.

Didymochlaena truncatula (Cloak Fern): leathery, brownish-green fronds; it grows well in dense shade.

Phlebodium aureum (Golden Polypody, Rabbit's-Foot Fern): eventually large, with a rather sprawling nature and mid-green fronds.

Polystichum auriculatum (Prickly Shield Fern): upright, tapering fronds with pointed ends.

GLOSSARY

Acaricide: Chemical used to kill mites, such as red spiders

Acid: Soils and composts with pH below 7.0

Aerial roots: Roots appearing from a stem above soil/compost level, e.g., Philodendrons, *Monstera deliciosa* (Swiss Cheese Plant), ivies and some orchids

Air layering: Method of propagating single-stemmed houseplants, such as *Ficus elastica* (Rubber Plant)

Alkaline: Soils and composts with pH above 7.0

Annual: Plant that completes its life cycle in a single year – seeds germinate, plants grow and produce flowers within one growing season

Anther: Part of a stamen, the male reproductive part of a flower

Aphids: Often known as greenfly, they cluster on stems, shoots, leaves, and flowers, sucking sap and causing damage

Areole: Unique to cacti, they are modified side-shoots in the form of small, cushion-like, usually raised areas; spines or hairs develop from them

Asexual: Non-sexual, sometimes used to refer to vegetative propagation, e.g., cuttings and division

Axil: Junction between leaf and stem, from where flower stems and side-shoots may develop

Biennial: Plant that makes its initial growth during one year and only flowers during the following year

Bleeding: Loss of sap from some plants after they are cut

Bloom: Two meanings: either a flower or a powdery covering

Bonsai: Art of growing dwarfed shrubs and trees in small containers

Bottle gardening: Growing plants indoors in enclosed environments created by large glass jars, e.g., carboys

Bottom heat: Warming of rooting mixture from below to encourage rapid root development

Botrytis: Fungal disease also known as gray mold

Bract: Modified leaf associated with flowers; some act as protection for a flower, others take the place of petals to become the main attraction, e.g., *Euphorbia pulcherrima* (Poinsettia)

Bud: Tightly packed, immature shoot or flower

Bulb: Food storage organ with a bud-like structure formed of fleshy scales attached at their bases to a basal plate, e.g., tulip

Bulbil: Immature miniature bulb, usually at the base of a bulb; some plants – e.g., *Asplenium bulbiferum* (Mother Fern) – have small plantlets on their leaves that are known as bulbils

Cactus: (plural: cacti) Succulent plants belonging to *Cactaceae* family; characterized by having areoles

Calcicole: Plant that likes lime

Calcifuge: Plant that dislikes lime

Calyx: Protective outer ring of flower parts, usually green

Capillary action: Passage of water upward through soil/potting compost: the finer the soil particles, the higher the rise of moisture (the same principle is used in self-watering systems)

Carboy: Large, round or pear-shaped glass bottle used as a container for plants

Cladode: Modified, flattened stem that takes the form and function of a leaf

Compost: Two meanings: the medium in which plants grow when in pots (known as potting soil in North America); material produced after decomposition of vegetable waste, which is then dug into the soil or used as a mulch

Corm: Swollen stem bases often classified with bulbs, but structurally different, e.g., crocuses, freesias

Crock: Piece of broken clay pot put in the base of a clay pot to prevent the drainage hole from becoming blocked

Cultivar: Plant produced in cultivation and indicating a "cultivated variety." Earlier, all variations, whether produced naturally in the wild or within cultivation, were known as "varieties"

Cutting: Vegetative method of increasing plants, by which a severed piece of a parent plant is encouraged to develop roots

Damping off: Disease that usually attacks seedlings soon after germination

Dead heading: Removal of dead or faded flowers to keep a plant tidy and encourage further flower development

Dibber: Rounded gardening tool for making holes; used for pricking out seedlings and inserting cuttings in seed-trays and pots

Division: Vegetative method of propagation involving root division

Epiphyte: Plant that grows on another but is not parasitic, e.g., some orchids and bromeliads

Fern: Perennial, flowerless plant that produces spores

Foliar feed: Fertilizer applied to foliage

Fronds: Leaves of a fern or palm

Fungicide: Chemical used to combat fungal diseases

Genus: Group of plants with similar botanical characteristics; within a genus are one or more species, each with slightly different characteristics

Germination: Process that occurs within a seed when given adequate moisture, air, and warmth; the seed-coat ruptures and a seed-leaf grows upward toward the light while a root develops and grows downward (to most gardeners, germination is when they see seed-leaves appearing through the surface of compost/soil)

Glochid: Small, hooked hair that grows on some cacti

Heel: Pieces of older wood attached to the base of some half-ripe (semi-mature, semi-hardwood) cuttings, which need to be trimmed to remove whisker-like growths

Humidity: Amount of moisture in the atmosphere – the higher the temperature, the more moisture air retains

Insecticide: Chemical that kills insects

Loam: Mixture of sand, clay, silt, and decomposed organic material

Mist-spraying: Using a sprayer to create a fine mist of clean water around plants to increase humidity

Neutral: Neither acid nor alkaline

Node: Leaf joint or position where a shoot grows from a stem or main branch

Offset: Young plant that arises naturally around its parent, e.g., some bromeliads, bulbs, and Houseleeks (*sempervivums*)

Peat: Partly decomposed vegetable material, usually acid, often used in potting and seed composts

Pesticide: Chemical compound for killing insects and other pests

Petiole: Leaf-stalk

pH: Logarithmic scale used to define the acidity or alkalinity of soil. Chemically, neutral is 7.0, with figures above indicating increasing alkalinity, and below increasing acidity. Most plants grow well at 6.5

Plantlet: An offset produced on a plant's leaves or stems

Pot bound: When a plant fills its container with roots and has no further room in which they can grow; it is usually repotted at this stage

Potting-on: Transfer of an established plant from one pot to another

Potting soil: American term for potting compost

Potting-up: Transfer of a young plant from a seed-tray into a pot

Pricking-out: Transfer of seedlings from a seed-tray into another seed-tray or pot to give them more space

Propagation: Raising of new plants

Repotting: Moving a plant that fills its existing pot with roots into a larger one

Rhizome: Horizontal stems, underground or partly above; may be slender (Lily-of-the-Valley) or thick and corrugated (Bearded Irises)

Root ball: The potting compost in which a houseplant grows, together with its roots

Seed leaf: First leaf (sometimes two) appearing after germination

Seedling: Young plant with a single, unbranched stem, produced after a seed germinates

Sharp sand: Sometimes known as concreting sand, it has particles with a sharp nature to ensure good drainage and aeration

Species: Group of plants that breed together and have the same characteristics. Species belong to a genus, which can be formed of one or more species. Within a species, there may be several cultivars

Stigma: Female part of a flower that receives pollen from the male part

Succulent: Any plant with thick, fleshy leaves

Top-dressing: Removal of compost from the surface of plants in large containers and replacing it with fresh compost. Plants are usually top-dressed because they are too large to be repotted into fresh compost and a larger pot

Urn: Leaves at the center of bromeliads that form "vases" through which plants can be watered and fed

Variety: see Cultivar

Vegetative propagation: Method of increasing plants, including division of roots, layering, and taking cuttings

INDEX

C

PHOTO CREDITS

ABOUT THE AUTHOR

DAVID SQUIRE studied botany and horticulture at the Hertfordshire College of Horticulture and the Royal Horticulture Society's Garden at Wisley, England, where he gained the Wisley Diploma in Horticulture. Also, he was awarded an NK Gould Memorial Prize for his collection of herbarium specimens of native plants, which has since been lodged with the Booth Museum of Natural History in Brighton, Sussex, England.

David has been an editorial staff member for several gardening magazines, book publishing companies, and part-work publishers and has written more than 85 gardening and natural history books, which have been translated into several languages and sold in 20 countries throughout the world.